Rafa Euba has worked as a consultant psychiatrist for over 20 years. He studied medicine in his native Basque Country and psychiatry in England and pioneered the use of non-invasive brain stimulation for the treatment of depression in the UK. The experience he gathered through a long career dedicated to the alleviation of psychological pain has coloured his perspectives on the concept of happiness. Rafa is happily married and has a daughter.

Every psychiatric patient included in this book is an amalgam of several different real patients. I have a duty of strict confidentiality, so I have merged and split their attributes. I have also changed their names and in some cases their sex, age, or other characteristics, and then added fictional elements so that any individual patient that contributed to each of these amalgams is completely and utterly unidentifiable as a result. Therefore, any resemblance to an actual person is, as they say, purely coincidental.

YOU are not MEANT to be HAPPY.

So stop trying

RAFA EUBA

CRUX
PUBLISHING

First published in the United Kingdom in 2021
by Crux Publishing Ltd.

ISBN: 978-1-913613-03-7

ACKNOWLEDGEMENTS

I am very grateful to Rachel, my wife, who very patiently helped me revise the manuscript; to Christopher, my very helpful and supportive publisher; to Catriona May, my dear friend, who gave me invaluable advice, and to Josephine Lethbridge, Matt Warren and Heather Kroeker, editors at *The Conversation,* the online publication where I first published some of the thoughts contained in this book. I am, of course, immensely grateful to all and each of my patients, who helped me understand my own emotions, my own fears and my own hopes.

To Lina

CONTENTS

INTRODUCTION

The ten trillion nerve connections in our brains do a lot of things. They smell a rose; they plan the cooking of a dish; they love; they remember a summer's day; they plot; they feel fear; they resolve a puzzle; they sing. They do all these things and many more. But they don't know how to make us happy.

Ten trillion is a lot of connections. There are this many because the brain has to process enormous amounts of information and take a large number of executive actions while burning a lot of energy. The brain governs everything in our lives, from adopting a posture to telling a joke; from writing a poem to regulating the body temperature. It carries out all these functions in a concerted and organised way in order to fulfil the mission with which it has been entrusted by its natural design: to make sure that we survive and reproduce. That's all. There is nothing in its brief about happiness.

Happiness is not natural. If it were, there would be no need to write instruction manuals on how to obtain it. It is a mere human construct, an abstract idea, absent from our actual human experience and devoid of a biological basis.

A huge happiness and positive thinking industry has helped create the fantasy that happiness is a realistic goal, something that is potentially inside us, if only we allow it to express itself, which is what would happen if we simply followed certain sets of instructions.

We are not meant to be happy, or even content. Instead, we are designed simply to survive and reproduce, like every other creature in the natural world. In fact a state of contentment is positively discouraged by Nature because it would lower our guard against possible threats to our survival. Happiness is an impossible project.

CHAPTER 1

THE FOURTEEN HAPPY DAYS OF THE CALIPH

Vladimir is a very charming Russian gentleman in his forties. He is, by any standards, a rich man, but not as rich as he would like to be. I meet him at my outpatients psychiatric clinic on a lovely early spring morning, in which my patients' depressions seem incongruent with the crispness of the light coming through the window.

"I am a failure, doctor."

He starts by looking at the floor with a very melancholic expression and moving his head sideways slowly. His voice is deep and resonant, dark and regretful. I see a lot of depressed people in my clinics and this kind of opening remark doesn't take me by surprise.

"I'm not sure why you say that," I reply, "after all, you have a good family, a social circle, and you have done very well for yourself with your car import business..."

"Are you kidding?" he interrupts, "all my friends have done better than me. Every single one of them has a private jet; out of the lot of us, I am the only one who doesn't have a jet. I am certainly a failure, I tell you!" Vladimir concludes sombrely.

I find myself feeling compassionate towards my patient's lack of a private jet and I feel for the distress this cruel deprivation has caused him. I, too, am poorer than I would like to be, so I have no difficulties sympathising with Vladimir, which is my duty anyway.

"I'm sorry to hear that," I say in a quiet voice, trying to sound comforting.

"It's alright doctor, I'm coming to terms with it."

The fact is that Vladimir, like me and like every other person on the planet, is very hard to satisfy. The jet plane, if he did get one, would not satisfy him. Millionaires, no matter their wealth, always want more money. This burning and relentless material ambition is one of the reasons why they are rich in the first place. Some millionaires have much more money than they could possibly spend, so their appetite for it isn't fuelled by a desire for more comforts or luxuries, but by their longing for money as an abstract, ethereal idea.

In Vladimir's case, he doesn't only regret a material deficit in the plane he never had; the empty tarmac, where the jet should be, also represents his own perceived personal failure.

Even if our appetite for wealth was satisfied, or tamed by overriding altruistic or spiritual beliefs, there are other desires to be fulfilled in our quest for happiness. It is obvious, for instance, that Vladimir's aeronautic dreams are based on an ambition to see himself as a successful man, not on an aspiration for more leg space and faster boarding times.

And yet, even when all those other needs are satisfied, a state of sustained happiness will still remain a theoretical and always elusive goal, as Abd-al-Rahman III, Caliph of Córdoba in the 10th century, discovered.

Abd-al-Rahman had it all. He was one of the most powerful men of his time and ruled Al-Andalus, in present day Southern Spain, for over fifty years, between his youth and his death in his seventies. Contemporary chroniclers noted his short stature (he had trouble reaching the stirrups when riding a horse). He owed his red beard (a defect he felt the need to correct by dyeing it black) and blue eyes to his Basque slave mother, but his paleness and unimpressive build did not prevent people thinking that he was good-looking.

His youth wasn't idyllic, especially if one considers that his father was murdered at the orders of Abd-al-Rahman's grandfather, an action that suggests a certain degree of dysfunctionality in the family.

He was admired for his political skill and for how dexterously and successfully he managed to encourage adherence to his rule and deter any possible challengers to his authority. He conquered much of the Iberian Peninsula and Al-Andalus's hitherto fragmented political base was repaired and consolidated. Córdoba, which sits some 80 miles inland from the coast, became the biggest and most important city in Europe. He endowed the city with some seventy libraries and a university, as well as a celebrated medical school. He encouraged and promoted culture and the arts in an atmosphere of tolerance between Muslims, Jews and Christians. His reign saw the works of the Greek masters translated into Arabic, establishing a link with Hellenistic culture. He also made himself the kind of palace he felt he deserved, the almost mythical Medina Azahara, a few miles away from Cordoba itself.

When finished, Medina Azahara became the quintessential Arabian Nights palace. To imagine it, one should visualise an Arab medieval version of the Forbidden City, at a time when most Europeans lived in hamlets that consisted of simple mud huts. This large and luxurious citadel, set in the foothills of Sierra Morena, in Southern Iberia, included royal residences, administrative buildings, baths and mosques, as well as two harems, one female and the other male, so Abd-al-Rahman would never have any trouble satisfying his eclectic appetites.

Abd-al-Rahman, was, in summary, a good-looking (if a little short), powerful, cultivated, respected, hedonistic and very rich man. He had however an anankastic type of personality, according to JA Vallejo-Nágera, a psychiatrist and historian who studied the psychological traits of the Caliph. In other words, he was a little "anal" and obsessive in his ways. As a result, he felt the need to analyse and document his life, including observations that in most other lives would go unrecorded. For instance, he made a note in his diary if a given day had been a happy one. Towards the end of his life, when he was having a tough time with a probable depressive illness and therefore not in the best of moods, he decided to count the exact number of days in which he recorded in his diary that he had felt happy. They amounted to precisely fourteen. This is how he put it:

"I have now reigned above fifty years in victory or peace; beloved by my subjects, dreaded by my enemies, and respected by my allies. Riches and honours, power and pleasure have waited on my call, nor does any earthly blessing appear to have been wanting to my felicity. In this situation, I have diligently numbered the days of pure and genuine happiness which have fallen to my lot: they amount to Fourteen: - O man! place not thy confidence in this present world!"

Of course, there is more to life than "*riches and honours, power and pleasure*". Happiness, if it does exist, must surely be an elevated entity for which the satisfaction of needs, itself a difficult objective, is a necessary but insufficient requirement. The "Maslow's hierarchy of needs" will help us illustrate this point.

Abraham Maslow was an American psychologist. He grew up in relative poverty in Brooklyn, the child of Ukrainian immigrants. He struggled in his personal life with issues such as racism (he was Jewish) and an awful relationship with his mother, whom he openly hated, so he was able to recognise that human wellbeing requires the satisfaction of material and psychological needs, which he stratified into a series of different levels, normally represented as a pyramid. He thought that more basic needs had to be satisfied before moving up to the next level – water and food before safety, then love, self-esteem and only then self-actualisation. But subsequent research shows that humans don't always follow this path in the anticipated order and that satisfying different levels of need either simultaneously, or in the "wrong order", doesn't seem to affect wellbeing significantly. This explains how those living in poor countries can also satisfy their psychological needs even when the fulfilment of more basic needs is uncertain.

"Self-actualisation", placed at the summit of the pyramid, occurs when a person has finally achieved his or her moral and creative potential. This theory was first published in the 1940s, but I remember it as being particularly popular when I was growing up in the Seventies, when every celebrity interviewed on TV claimed to have self-actualisation as their personal goal. It sounded a bit pompous and a tad narcissistic.

This brings us back to Abd-al-Rahman. His alleged appetites for young people, as the story of St Pelagius[1] illustrates, suggests that he may have neglected the moral dimension of his own self-actualisation, although any Spanish legends of the period involving a Muslim villain and a saintly Christian must be taken with a pinch of salt. His emphasis on "*riches and honours, power and pleasure*" also suggests a certain excessive focus on himself, perhaps in common with those self-absorbed TV personalities who sought self-actualisation. It is possible therefore that had Abd-al-Rahman been more morally sound

1 Pelagius of Córdoba was a 13-year-old Christian boy from the north of the peninsula, renowned for his piety and beauty, who was held captive by Abd-al-Rahman and who, according to legend, was tortured and dismembered by the ruler when Pelagius rejected both his sexual advances and his demand that he converted to Islam. He became a saint, as well as the religious inspiration for Franco's fascist regime in the 20th century.

and altruistic, this might have resulted in him reaching self-actualisation, which in turn would have allowed him to enjoy countless happy days in his life and not just fourteen. However, out of the list of personal characteristics Maslow identified in "actualisers", which to be honest reads like a list of attributes he rather liked on a person, or even a lonely hearts ad, *- spontaneous, natural, profound relationships, sense of humour, compassionate, etc.-* Abd-al-Rahman in fact fulfilled a few of them, according to his contemporaries. Moreover, the causal link between self-actualisation and happiness is conceptually tenuous and, more importantly, Maslow himself believed that only a small number of people – single digit percentages – would reach a state of self-actualisation. In any case, it is clear that he felt that most of us are not self-actualised, and probably will never be. This almost unachievable target is reminiscent of other near-impossible nirvanas, like, Nirvana itself, Nietzsche's Superman status, or the Jehovah's Witnesses' paradise.

Maslow died comparatively young at 62 of a heart attack, presumably self-actualised.

I see Vladimir in clinic a few months later. He has brought me a box of Ferrero Rocher chocolates. This time he seems a little more cheerful. I attribute his improvement in mood to the cognitive-behavioural psychotherapy he is receiving from one of our psychologists and to the antidepressant tablet I prescribed for him. To be honest, when a depressed patient improves, it is often impossible to know what did the trick, or even if they simply got better spontaneously. This is called a "regression to the mean", which simply means that over a period of time things are likely to normalise and approach the average. This is the reason, incidentally, why new football managers tend to do better initially than their failing predecessors, who eventually would also have started to win matches again anyway[2].

"The therapy is helping me identify what's important in life and what isn't," he starts. "I realise now that I was too fixated on the ideas of success and failure and on material stuff being the indicator of whether I had succeeded or failed."

He says all this with the conviction of the man who has realised the error of his ways and seen the light. I nod approvingly. We both agree, material wealth and luxuries are shallow and superficial, other values are better at measuring success, etc.

"I need to tell you something though, doctor." His face has now adopted a critical, disappointed expression.

"What is it?"

"That Casio watch you wear. It's cheap and nasty. C'mon, surely a doctor like you can do better than that!"

---

2 RH Frank explains this point in *The Economic Naturalist*.

CHAPTER 2

EVOLUTION

Gustave Flaubert was of the opinion that the three necessary conditions for happiness were stupidity, selfishness and a good health. Of the three, stupidity was the most important, he thought. Instead, evolution seems to have bequeathed us with intelligence, altruism, and fragile health. It certainly prioritised the development of a big frontal lobe in our brain (which gives us excellent executive and analytical skills) over a natural ability to be happy. This tells us a lot about Nature's priorities.

Nature promotes those biological characteristics that favour survival and reproduction and discourages those that don't. Not by will or design, but by means of natural selection, as Charles Darwin stipulated in the 19th century. Unfortunately, Nature doesn't select the happiest individuals, but the fittest, in an evolutionary process that highlights fear and discourages contentment. Our chronically unhappy species is the product of such a process.

My patients' pain frequently reminds me of how adept humans are at suffering. We are so good at it because suffering is something that comes to us naturally.

It's a cold winter morning, so I know that inside the Victorian building where I sometimes see my patients will be freezing. Old hospitals never want to let go of their frigidity, as if doing so would betray the memories of the suffering contained within their walls. The first patient in today's clinic list is a very pleasant gentleman in his eighties, whom I know well. He is slim, tall and elegant, and suffers with that curse that afflicts us all, and the old in particular: loneliness.

Frank has been tormented by his downstairs neighbour for years. He is alone in the world and, being alone, he feels vulnerable and threatened by his neighbour's constant complaints to the council, accusing Frank of having a very noisy dog that barks day and night. Milou, his small female white terrier, is Frank's only companion in life. The complaints, and the worry that he may have to get rid of his dog, have made him quite depressed and in need of antidepressant tablets and psychotherapy.

When Frank enters the room, I worry. He is normally able to smile and show a certain amount of warmth, but not today. Today he talks in a quiet voice, avoids eye contact and seems reluctant to tell me what's wrong.

"It's my neighbour," he finally says.

My initial thought is that his neighbour must have succeeded at last in her demands that Frank gets rid of Milou.

"She's died."

"Your dog has died?"

"No, not my dog, my neighbour has died. And she was the only person who ever talked to me, only to complain, that's true, but now she's gone I'll feel even lonelier."

Now, it is fair to say that Frank isn't a very sunny type of character. He doesn't have the most optimistic, half-full glass personality and he is genuinely alone in the world, except for his little terrier. But he is nevertheless a good example of how our design predisposes us to find fault in our lives, to scan for trouble. Frank's keen eye for the negative is what Psychology calls "negativity bias", which affects us all to a certain extent, even at the most cheerful end of the half-glass spectrum. Our negativity bias is the reason behind the fact that newspapers are always full of bad news and novels and films full of absolutely horrible pathos. Even *The Sound of Music* has Nazis in it. Bad stuff, change, instability and threats simply grab our attention much more strongly than a state of insipid placidity. We see the little stain in the dress, the blemish in our skin, spot the flaw in someone's character, and those imperfections stand out in our conscience, crisp, distinct and grossly disproportionate in relation to all the accompanying virtue and harmony, which go unnoticed.

I arrive home early and allow my mind to wonder aimlessly, which is never a good thing. I then observe a thin, tiny crack in the plaster in the wall of my bathroom, obviously too small and insignificant to constitute proof of subsidence. And yet, in my mind, while I assess the issue, looking at the crack studiously and wondering if I should add it to my ever expanding list of worries, the crack is the most important attribute of my house. My house has turned into a tiny wall crack with a building attached to it.

This negativity bias is itself anchored in our need to identify and try to neutralise threats in order to improve our chances of survival.

Imagine a perfectly happy individual who is constantly satisfied, enjoying the many little pleasures that life can offer. His job is a little monotonous and predictable, as a more complex occupation would inevitably generate happiness-corrupting anxieties and frictions. This man doesn't want to have a better job (fair enough), so he doesn't worry about others being promoted before him. He has a good relationship with his partner, so he is not bothered by feelings of jealousy or boredom in her company. So far, so good. But then, one morning our man finds a lump in his testicle. Unable to feel worry or anxiety, he quickly concludes that it is probably nothing. He dies of testicular cancer soon after, childless. He was only 25.

The point of this little sad story is that we need anxiety to help us survive and reproduce. We need to be on our guard and scrutinise ourselves and our surroundings for potential perils. Satisfaction and containment won't do. Fear and anxiety keep us on our toes, together with other negative emotions, such as anger, pain and disgust, which also have life-saving functions because they too help us avoid and repel dangers, and in the case of pain, recoil from whatever is inflicting it, while letting us know that something is wrong.

To be fair, positive emotions also have an essential role in survival. Calories in our food, a warm shelter, safety, material possessions and the attentions of a sexual partner, are all rewarded with pleasure and a sense of wellbeing. Food and sex are important, but so is any other factor that may be ultimately associated with survival and reproduction. For instance, cementing one's position in a social group feels reassuring because the support of this group will help with the task of living long enough to pass on our genes successfully. The joy of altruism, camaraderie, family life and companionship all help the tribe and therefore the individuals in it. Even the enjoyment of entertainment can be understood as a way of creating common myths and values that will bond the group together. Other pleasures, such as the appreciation of beauty, may be more difficult to explain as an evolutionary advantage. Nevertheless, even if some of the things that we feel and do were epiphenomena or by-products in terms of survival, it is still clear that a great part of who we are can be understood in terms of the need to make it to adulthood and then have as many offspring as possible.

So we need both positive and negative emotions to survive. This doesn't sound too bad. In fact it sounds balanced and reasonable, something one can easily accept and live with. Except that there is a crucial component built into the dynamic that exists between positive and negative feelings, something that upsets the balance between them, tilting the scales in the wrong direction: what I am referring to is the fact that positive emotions, unlike the negative ones, are ephemeral and fizzle out after a while, leaving the individual chronically unsatisfied and perpetually in need of new rewards. This imbalance makes dissatisfaction our *default* position. We feel forever in need and always wanting, and yet our disposition to feel fear and pain remains constant and indefatigable.

Any measure of happiness that we may experience is, in any case, inconstant. Happiness has been compared to *"a feather flying in the air: it flies light, but not for very long"*, as Brazilian poet Vinicius de Moraes put it. In its teasing elusiveness it has also been compared to a capricious butterfly, which *"when pursued, is always just beyond your grasp, but which, if you will sit down quietly, may alight upon you"*, in a possibly apocryphal quote, attributed to Nathaniel Hawthorne, the 19th century American novelist.[3] Guy de Maupassant, the celebrated writer, is one of the residents in Montparnasse Cemetery in Paris. He chased the flying feather of ephemeral joy: *"I have coveted everything and taken pleasure in nothing"*, says his epitaph. The coveting of everything may have had something to do with the fact that he ended up in Montparnasse cemetery as a result of the syphilis that he contracted in the pursuit of those pleasures.

I arrive at home, tired and weary after a whole day of listening to the sufferings of others. It is now even colder than in the morning and the wet darkness that envelopes everything

3 Hawthorne was a descendant of the Salem witch trials judge, someone upon whom the merry butterfly of happiness probably never alighted.

matches my drained spirits. The good news I find in the post provides a dissonant but welcome note: I had applied to receive a certain minor recognition, while fearing at the same time a painful rejection, and the outcome is better than I had hoped. I had worried about this for a while and fantasised that a positive outcome would induce in me a more or less permanent ecstasy of joy. I am certainly rejoiced by the news, but while relaxing with a glass of wine in my hand, celebrating my very small triumph, my mind wanders towards the crack in the wall I noticed earlier. Could it be serious perhaps?

Many believe that our chronic dissatisfaction is the result of our materialism. This belief is consistent with the widespread myth that ascribes unhappiness to the shallowness, stresses and tribulations of modern life. The idea is undoubtedly persuasive, and yet the uncontroversial truth is that humanity has always suffered. In fact, one could argue that it is, if anything, surprising that suffering is still with us, as strong as ever, given that we are now so much more comfortable and safer than we were in preindustrial times. Considering that most of us don't have to worry about having food and medicines, or even entertainment, one would expect the weight of suffering that had historically oppressed humanity to be gradually easing. But it isn't, and the reason it isn't is that we carry that weight inside us, in our genetic design.

The constancy of human misery across space and time is striking. Fleeting joy, as well as cruel melancholia, have been with us ever since Adam and Eve left the Garden of Eden. Hippocrates postulated that a sad temperament was induced by having too much black bile, which is what the word "melancholia" literally means. References to the miseries of earthly life abound in Middle Ages chronicles; a 17th century Oxford scholar called Robert Burton even felt the need to write a whole volume on the subject of melancholia and all sad things, which was hugely popular at the time. In fact, the smile is a recently discovered feature. Our ancestors preferred to be portrayed looking very serious, their facial expression congruent with the seriousness and general sadness of life.

One would assume that the distress associated with a financial crisis is something peculiar to this century, but not even this is new. The so-called "Long Depression" hit the British economy very severely towards the end of the 19th century. *The Times* reported in 1880 that *business anxiety* had become a leading cause of suffering and even insanity: "to *business anxiety* are to be attributed no fewer than 24 cases, being half as often again as this cause ever before appeared in the [Royal Edinburgh] asylum [admission] list."

There is no escaping from suffering in either space or time. It is ubiquitous and omnipresent because it is in our nature, and we can thank our genetic design for that.

Not that evolution and natural selection have any particular plans. Evolution doesn't want to go anywhere. It certainly doesn't want to go anywhere *better*. It happens randomly as a result of mutations, which are nothing but mistakes in the replication of the DNA. So the idea that we humans are "more evolved" than other animals is misleading. A microbe is as good at being a microbe as a human is at being a human. And if you are hoping that evolution will eventually weed out our chronic dissatisfaction and anxieties and make, if not us, at least our distant descendants happier, well, that's not going to happen, as there is no drive or reason in Nature to pursue that particular project. In any case, since we are now able to control our own survival and reproduction, we are no longer subject to the pressures of natural selection. This means that we are not evolving in any real sense of the word.

Many people find the idea of a random and mechanical evolutionary process occurring in the context of an impersonal and aloof universe challenging. They would prefer to think that what they see in the natural world is the result of some sort of plan and design. Perhaps this plan was executed by God, or otherwise by esoteric agents (like in the New Age philosophies), or even by Nature itself, or a combination of these. Most religious people don't have a problem with the Theory of Evolution and only a minority subscribe to an Old Testament creationist view of the world, and yet, at a deeper level, Nature's lack of purpose remains a problematic issue. For some, this is not just problematic, but simply inconceivable. They believe that naturally occurring events must necessarily have a purpose. This cognitive style has been termed "teleological thinking". A researcher at the University of Fribourg has found that creationists and those who believe in conspiracy theories share this particular way of understanding the world. They may believe, for instance, that the Sun rises *in order to* give us light, rather than simply because the laws of physics that govern the solar system demand it. Teleological thinking insists in finding a purpose where there is none.

Long before Darwin, Jean-Baptiste Lamarck, who was an 18th century French naturalist, had already postulated his own theory of evolution. This theory allowed a certain element of will and purpose in the evolutionary process because Lamarck believed, as did many others at the time, that a given characteristic that one had acquired in life could be passed on to the next generation. Similarly, those traits that one hadn't used in life could be eventually lost and not passed on to one's progeny. Curiously, Sigmund Freud himself advocated Lamarckism as a basis for some of his theories, specifically his belief that one could inherit traumatic memories from one's parents. Instead, our current understanding of evolution, based on Darwin's theory, is that animals (including ourselves, of course) evolve their traits through a process of competition and selection. In this process, spontaneous genetic mutations that, by chance, happen to be good for survival are more likely to make it to the next generation, whereas those that aren't will die out, together with the individuals carrying them. So, for instance, a mutation that contributed towards the development of that very analytical frontal lobe in our brain, in combination with many other mutations and therefore in a very slow and stepwise manner, finally produced a highly sophisticated brain that helped our ancestors relate more effectively to the physical environment in which they lived. The power of their frontal lobe allowed these humans to assess, plan and make decisions, and to do this in co-operation with other individuals in a complex social group. In this way, they were able to adapt even to the most hostile environments. The children of these primitive humans were better fed and better protected and therefore more likely to survive and reproduce, blessing the next generation with the genes that had accidentally given them a bigger brain. This is how our oversized frontal lobe became an evolutionary advantage and therefore stayed in our genetic code.

A creationist would believe that our big frontal lobe was designed from scratch by an "intelligent designer", whereas a follower of Lamarck would see an intention and a will in the transmission of certain traits and the loss of others down the generations. Either approach would find it difficult to accept that our big brain is the result of myriad genetic accidents, in which the main criterion for the success of each of those random errors was whether it promoted survival and reproduction or not.[4]

In the context of natural selection, the individual doesn't really matter very much. Only the species matters. That's why

4 The technical aspects of Evolution are, to be fair, a little more complex than this. Nevertheless, they invariably involve a process of natural (and sexual) selection serving the preservation of the species, which is pretty much purposeless and random.

we still have terrible teeth and weak coronary arteries. These "design" defects can be awful drawbacks for a given person, but teeth and hearts tend to give us serious problems only after we have reproduced and, by then, our duty to the species has already been fulfilled.

Nature simply does not care about the wellbeing of the individual. If a given mutation advanced the interests of the species only one iota, but at the cost of enormous suffering for each of the members that constituted that species, then Nature would not hesitate a moment before favouring that mutation. Admittedly, it might be hard to imagine a mutation that would be advantageous overall and yet involve so much suffering, but the basic principle of the supremacy of the interests of the species over those of the individual still holds true. Evolution, whether we like it or not, is not driven by a need to optimise the individual's wellbeing.

We have already commented on how feeling anxious can favour survival. Feeling depressed, as long as this doesn't reach a pathological intensity, can also be seen as an evolutionary adaptation. Experts in this field argue that Nature's failure to get rid of depression in the evolutionary process is due precisely to the fact that depression as an adaptation plays a useful role in times of adversity. This is a curious thought, given that one of the first things depression does is lower the libido, or even inhibit it altogether, and without a libido nothing much is going to happen in terms of reproduction. If it gets much worse, it can also have an adverse effect on one's physical health, increasing the likelihood of developing all sorts of diseases, from heart attacks to cancer. It is a well-established fact that people who struggle with depression have shorter lives than the rest of the population. So here we have something that affects our chances of both survival and reproduction directly, and yet,

Nature appears to want us to get depressed in times of adversity, as if there was an advantage in this.

And it seems that there is. Depression helps the depressed individual disengage from hopeless situations in which he or she cannot win. Perseverance has a value, but it also has a significant cost. If every attempt to woo that elusive potential partner, or get that promotion, results in utter failure, then perhaps the time has come to recalibrate one's self-esteem downwards (a typical feature of depression) and start feeling depressed. Perhaps I am not, after all, attractive enough to win the affections of a woman like her, or competent enough to go any higher in the occupational ladder. This recalibration, together with the acceptance that the desired goals will never be achieved, will be painful, but in the long run the readjusted individual will meet a partner who is in his own sexual attraction league and will function occupationally at his level of competence. The acceptance of one's appropriate sexual and tribal status will be a good thing for the group and therefore, ultimately, for the individual too, and it will have been achieved through a period of depressed adjustment.

People facing adversity also ruminate a lot, which is another typical feature in depression. Their thoughts go round and round, often very painfully, trying to find a way out of their worries. Some evolutionary thinkers believe that this is an expression of how we are meant to find logical solutions to difficult problems. It will be the wrong strategy for a person who is actually facing an insoluble problem because, as we have just seen, persevering in the face of impossible odds is a bad idea. However, having the determination and the need to find a logical solution to a problem is indeed imprinted in our human design and, when applied generally to our species as a whole, this drive will resolve many problems that could otherwise have threatened our survival. External signs of psychological distress, like crying, or looking sad, are also thought to elicit care and attention from others in the group, to the benefit of the distressed person. It is important to bear in mind however that we are talking here about brief periods of psychological adjustment, rather than prolonged and serious depressive episodes, which are not directly favoured by natural selection and will have a detrimental effect on survival and reproduction. Besides, the looking sad and crying a lot strategy, if sustained for a long time, will eventually become a tad weary to others. At any rate, these depressive adjustments illustrate quite effectively how a person feeling bad can be good for the genetic success of humankind.

I see Frank again a few months later. He is a little better than the last time he came to clinic, but remains generally downcast. He tells me in his warm and steady voice about his daily life, which he finds dreary and devoid of purpose. Still, he takes one day at the time and soldiers on, as one must, he says. But it has been hard lately, what with his enemy/companion downstairs passing away and then Milou developing a mysterious ailment, which luckily resolved spontaneously, but resulted in some big bills at the vet's.

"And then also..."

Frank hesitates; there had been some other adversity, but he can't remember it right now.

"Oh yes," he finally recalls, visibly satisfied, "I went to see the blood specialist and he told me I've got leukaemia. He says the leukaemia explains why I'd been feeling so worn-out."

Frank abandons this subject immediately and proceeds to comment on all the other defects and disappointments he finds in his daily life, chief amongst them the fact that "there is nothing on telly worth watching these days".

A cognitive distortion, I think at first. Frank is minimising the importance of his diagnosis and protecting himself through denial. And yet, who is to say, I reflect a moment later, that the news about his leukaemia should be ranked higher than the other, apparently more mundane issues Frank has been struggling with lately? Perhaps I don't fully appreciate the significance of Milou's illness and Frank's neighbour dying. And what would be the point of denial, anyway, if he was still feeling depressed?

Feeling bad, at least intermittently, is what we do. So much so, that a state of happiness was found to be clearly pathological by Richard Bentall, a senior lecturer in clinical psychology at Liverpool University, back in 1992. He argued this point in a tongue in cheek article, which was nonetheless as logical as it was persuasive. Happiness, he wrote, meets all reasonable criteria for a psychiatric disorder: "It is statistically abnormal [...] and it is associated with various cognitive abnormalities - in particular, a lack of contact with reality". He was of the opinion that happiness "should be included in future editions of the major diagnostic manuals under the new name: major affective disorder, pleasant type". The lack of contact with reality is probably what Flaubert was referring to when he said that one needs to be stupid in order to be happy.

Could it be possible that we are truly condemned to a life of dissatisfaction, with only occasional flashing glimpses of contentment? Could Nature really be so unkind? Surely not. We all admire Nature in its complexity and beauty, and many believe that there is an inherent balance in the natural world that we humans have unsettled. It is this imbalance that makes us unhappy, according to this belief system. If only we obeyed the wishes of Nature, all would be well. This is compelling, except that Nature does not wish anything because it is not a person.

Humans have personified Nature for centuries. Diana of Ephesus, the Greek goddess represented with multiple breasts, lions on her arms and bees on her skirt, is one of the earliest examples of this personification. She originated in Turkey, was adopted by the Greeks and eventually became very popular all over Europe. In my native Basque Country, we had the pre-roman *Ama Lur*, or "Mother Earth", as a maternal deification of Nature. Nowadays, we encounter frequent references to Nature in many products we consume. These references are often intertwined with vague ethical statements and they always show Nature as a wise and benign entity, as long as we agree to follow and obey her, of course. The role God used to play in the past seems to have been transferred to Nature in our current secular society. Some of her unconditional supporters have in fact adopted a curiously preachy tone when they proselytise about her virtues. And yet death and illness are the most natural of events, often prevented by perfectly artificial medical interventions, so an untamed Nature cannot possibly be that good after all, or at least, not that good *for us*.

A complementary idea to Nature as a noble entity is that of primitive man as a noble entity: the "Noble Savage". This is a concept that tends to be associated with the French Enlightenment philosopher Jean-Jacques Rousseau, even though he didn't invent it. The basis of this belief was described by a French historian called Paul Hazard as follows: "The Savage obeys the will of Nature, his kindly mother, therefore he is happy. It is civilised folk who are the real barbarians". The myth of the Noble Savage was born with the age of exploration, when new cultures were being discovered, but the Europeans explorers didn't know enough about them yet to realise that these "savages" were just as human as they were, for better and for worse. They were just as generous and intelligent, but also just as envious, spiteful and violent as them. Dickens, in the 19th century, knew this and ridiculed the whole idea: "...if we have anything to learn from the Noble Savage, it is what to avoid. His virtues are a fable; his happiness is a delusion". We can conclude therefore that, regardless of whether we enter a state of constant harmony with Mother Nature, or otherwise regress to a state of noble savageness, happiness will remain always elusive. Expecting that Nature will help us in our quest for happiness will be futile.

The ultimate function of all the wonders in the biological world and of the evolutionary process is to maintain life through a cycle of conception and death of countless insignificant individuals, and not, however much we would like to believe it, to ensure that these individuals enjoy their short existence on this planet.

Richard Dawkins has said that there is in the universe we observe "no design, no purpose, no evil, no good, nothing but pitiless indifference". This thought certainly won't cheer you up, but accepting that Nature is not a loving mother watching over you, that she has indeed built into your genetic code an inability to be happy, and accepting too that we are all abandoned children of the universe, will help you put the inevitable miseries of your life in perspective. You are not letting Nature down by being sad. She couldn't care less.

CHAPTER 3

PERSONALITY

Personality affects wellbeing in a very significant way, but there is more to this interaction than a mere distinction between the cheerful and the gloomy. Having this or that personality will affect your periods of relative happiness, as well as your unhappiness, and how they are both experienced and manifested.

A few months ago I received a commission to write an article on this very topic, in which I used the example of Don Quixote, the idealistic and deluded knight, and Sancho Panza, his earthy page, to illustrate some basic personality parameters. They are the main characters in Miguel de Cervantes' famous 17th century novel.

In this story, Don Quixote's sensation-seeking and restless personality, as well as his lofty ideals, are the drivers of his misguided adventures. Unable to find excitement in the comfortable but mundane daily life of a landed country gentleman, he sets out to right all the wrongs in the world in the most chivalrous and valiant manner he can imagine, in a desire to emulate the romantic heroic knights he has come to admire in the fictional stories he devours day and night. His ambitious goals are unobtainable, though, and so he remains chronically dissatisfied.

In contrast, Sancho's goals, which are essentially some cheese and wine after each of their misadventures, are simple, and they are also reliable and immediately achievable. Sancho will inevitably have some difficult emotions, like every other human, that will prevent him from being consistently happy. But he will be less inclined to express his occasional periods of distress in complex existential terms.

On one level, then, Sancho's personality seems better suited than Don Quixote's for achieving a degree of psychological wellbeing. But we need to consider the fact that Don Quixote's tortured loftiness will also afford him occasional moments of ecstasy that Sancho will never experience.

Don Quixote has a type of personality that Galen, the Greek physician of classical times, would have labelled as "choleric": passionate, charismatic, impulsive and sensation seeking. He also has an extremely rich, but equally unstable, inner life, which produces copious amounts of fantasy and emotion.

The extroverted are happier

Soon after the Second World War, a London-based psychologist called Hans Eysenck developed a personality theory that included the dimensions of "extroversion" and "neuroticism". Quixote is high in extroversion (he engages constantly with the external world) and high in neuroticism (his emotional life is unstable and intense), a combination that would be the equivalent of Galen's choleric personality.

Sancho is, of course, the exact opposite. He could be described as "phlegmatic" in Galen's classification: he is generally introverted, and being perfectly steady in emotional terms, he would certainly score very low on neuroticism. He does not view the world through the filter of a rich but volatile inner life, and instead sees ordinary windmills where Quixote sees formidable giants.

Personality types have been found to be predictors of psychological wellbeing in a way that could be considered relatively intuitive. Essentially, there is a positive correlation between happiness and extroversion and a negative one between happiness and neuroticism. There may be a slight distorting element built into the assumption that extroverts are happier, in that a reflective introvert may perhaps be more likely to recognise and label unhappiness when it happens than those who are more focused on the world outside. Quixote is more neurotic than Sancho, but he is also more extroverted. The two will find and experience intermittent moments of happiness in different ways.

It seems therefore that what we need to be reasonably happy is a stable (low neuroticism) and outgoing (extrovert) character. Those of us who see ourselves as a little more neurotic than we would ideally like – and perhaps not quite as sociable as some others – can find comfort in the knowledge that a busy and lively inner life, coupled with an inquisitive nature, can be associated with certain types of creativity.

Peak experiences

The idea of happiness as a state of placidity and serenity, facilitated by a stable and untroubled psychological makeup, is persuasive, but it ignores perhaps the upper and more intense limits of human experience – and these have a power all their own. Maslow called them "peak experiences" and described them as "exciting, oceanic, deeply moving [and] even mystic and magical", and other superlative adjectives. Examples could be the feelings aroused by practising extreme sports, or contemplating particularly stirring works of art. The point is that some peculiarly animated temperaments are tormented by intense negative emotions, but, at the same time, this inner sparkle also makes them receptive to the beauty of the world and more likely to experience the vivid passions associated with certain unusual experiences. By definition, these peak experiences will only happen rarely.

Feeling in control

Don Quixote is a dissatisfied man and his ambitions to achieve his glorious goals are always frustrated. He has, however, certain characteristics that have been found to be associated with happiness: an optimistic "attributional style" and an internal "locus" (place) of control.

Don Quixote's "internal locus of control" means that he feels in charge of his destiny (despite all the evidence to the contrary). Control resides within him. His optimistic "attributional style", meanwhile, refers to the fact that he always ascribes his failures to external forces, rather than to permanent internal issues. He feels he has the ability to control his fate, and when something goes wrong (which in his case happens all the time), it's due to temporary issues that won't affect his chances of success in his next adventure. Successes are his doing; failures have nothing to do with him.

Sancho, on the other hand, has a reactive attitude to life. He doesn't have any fantasies about being in control of his destiny, which he believes is in the lap of the gods. "The lucky man has nothing to worry about," he says.

So, in this respect at least, Don Quixote, driving his own fortune and making his own luck, is probably happier in his quest, however frustrating, than Sancho is in his passive contentment.

Belly size

Is it significant that lofty Quixote is tall and slim, whereas Sancho is short and stocky and has a generous belly[5]? In other words, are certain physical types associated with jollier (and therefore perhaps happier) personalities?

Ernst Kretschmer was a German psychiatrist who thought that there was an association between physique and personality. He called people with a slim build "asthenics" and thought that they were more likely to have a detached, solitary and generally odd personality (Quixote), while those with a heftier type of physique and abdomens (Sancho) he called "pyknics" and considered them to be more likely to have a warm and gregarious personality. In other words, happier. Falstaff, a recurring character in Shakespeare's plays and subsequent operas, is another example of a chubby and jolly character that personifies this archetype. Kretschmer's theory on body types isn't taken very seriously these days, and yet these physical archetypes persist, so one can't help wondering if there may be perhaps an element of truth in them.

Narcissism

Don Quixote appears to have a very high opinion of himself, perhaps even a "superiority complex". He sees himself as a singular and exceptional kind of man, the sort that will carry out the most amazing feats in the most brave, just, selfless and elegant way. One would assume that having such a high opinion of oneself would be a good thing, as far as feeling happy is concerned, but Alfred Adler, another celebrated German

5 "Panza" means belly is Spanish.

speaking 20th century psychologist, postulated that apparent feelings of superiority are often an over-compensation for an underlying but unconscious "inferiority complex". So perhaps Quixote feels inadequate underneath it all and fancies himself as the ultimate romantic knight as a way of compensating for that inadequacy.

Don Quixote's high opinion of himself might also be a sign of narcissism. We all know a narcissist. They fancy themselves, they seek admiration (and of course think they deserve it), they exploit others and lack empathy. They are vain and arrogant. They are not very likeable, in short. We comfort ourselves thinking that these ugly attributes surely represent some sort of over-compensation, like in the case of Adler's "superiority complex", that they are poor insecure and unhappy creatures underneath their self-inflated nastiness, that even if they don't show empathy themselves, we should perhaps be empathetic with their psychological shortcomings. Disturbingly, however, there is some empirical evidence that narcissists are in fact a pretty happy bunch. They are happier than the rest of us, according to research carried out at Queen's University Belfast, because their self-adoring traits shield them from a variety of unpleasant emotions. It could be argued that the current self-branding and selfie social media culture promotes narcissism, but far from shielding anybody from unpleasant emotions, this pressure to sell oneself socially as a desirable product every day of the year creates instead enormous psychological stresses.

But I think it would be unfair to label poor Quixote as a narcissist. He is too likeable.

IQ

Many of the stresses we have to endure are due to the need to adapt to the ever changing circumstances in our lives. This suggests that a good level of intelligence – a high IQ – which would enable us to understand, process and then adapt to the challenges we find in our life trajectories, would help us be happy. We saw in the chapter on evolution how Nature gave us an intelligent brain, which is in fact good at doing these understanding and processing tasks, but not good at all at making us happy, at least directly. To expand this a little, there is in fact evidence that a higher IQ will make you feel better in yourself, but this is simply because this higher IQ will afford you better chances in life (a university education, for instance), which will in turn place you at a higher stratum in the social divide. It is this higher social status, with everything else that it entails, that will buy you more happiness, not the higher IQ itself. It is obvious however that neither a high level of intellectual sophistication nor even a higher social status in itself will guarantee happiness, and in Quixote's case they clearly don't.

Emotional intelligence

There may be a stronger correlation between "emotional" intelligence and wellbeing than between this and regular, raw intelligence. Emotional intelligence is the kind of difficult stuff we constantly process that has nothing to do with understanding numbers or complicated arguments. It is to do instead with things like self-awareness, impulse control, persistence, motivation, empathy and social deftness, as Daniel Goleman explains in his best-selling book on this subject.[6] There is a surprising amount of evidence supporting the notion that being good at these "soft" tasks predicts wellbeing. Conversely, a lack of emotional intelligence is a major handicap, one that will pose countless obstacles and difficulties for the person affected and those around them. And yet, promoting and nurturing emotional intelligence won't make our lives better necessarily. Emotional intelligence is, as so many other things in life, good or bad depending on the context. A study conducted at the University of Central Florida that looked at the relationship between emotional intelligence and work performance found that if the job in question required emotional instincts, such as working as a door to door salesman, then having emotional skills helped performance, but curiously, if the job was of the drier sort in terms of emotional demands, such as mechanics or accountants, then being an emotional genius was a liability. No-one likes a touchy-feely accountant, not on the job anyway, even less an exuberant or mercurial airline pilot.

Obviously, Don Quixote doesn't exactly excel on emotional intelligence.

It is clear therefore that neither Quixote's nor Sancho's personality type will ensure or even facilitate happiness. Personality factors and temperamental attitudes are important, but as we have seen, they don't operate in a single dimension of placidity versus psychological restlessness, extraversion versus introversion, or even optimism versus pessimism. Admittedly, extroversion, low neuroticism, an internal *locus* of control, an optimistic attributional style, achievable goals in life, and a good level of emotional intelligence, will all be better than

6 Goleman D, 2006. *Emotional Intelligence: Why It Can Matter More Than IQ*.

their opposites, but not even this very rare combination would guarantee that one would manage to enjoy Maslow's "peak experiences", or even develop a sense of meaning and purpose, or, for that matter, that one will have the luck in life that a reasonable level of wellbeing demands.

Given that a state other than happiness ("unhappiness" sounds a little harsh) is inevitable, it is more useful to look at personality not as something that will determine our level of happiness, but rather as a factor that will channel and manifest our mixed, changeable and often difficult emotions in our own particular, idiosyncratic and occasionally charming way.

CHAPTER 4

THE BIOLOGY OF UNHAPPINESS

Only in exceedingly rare cases nowadays do neurosurgeons deliberately sever some of the connections between the limbic system and the frontal lobe of the brain. This used to be called a lobotomy. Psychosurgery, as we prefer to call it now, is reserved for very unusual cases of very extreme and absolutely constant and intense suffering that don't respond to any other interventions at all. This definition used to include many more people in the old days, before the advent of effective drugs, when all psychiatrists could do for their distressed patients was to send them to sleep with a very crude tranquilliser, or perhaps induce a diabetic coma, in the hope that this would somehow reset the brain to a better configuration. When I was a young trainee in psychiatry, back in the late 1980s, it wasn't unusual to see old lobotomy scars in the temples of very chronic patients. One of these patients was Rosa.

Rosa was in her mid-sixties when I knew her. She had pale blue eyes and a mild smile, a bit like Mona Lisa's, that permanently adorned her face. She had been an in-patient in a number of long-stay wards in a very old-fashioned asylum for many years. Nobody could tell how many exactly, as her original admission records had been lost. Hospital wards of this kind were being gradually emptied and closed down during my trainee years. Sometimes, only one or two wards remained open in a whole asylum, making the empty corridors and deserted grounds feel particularly spooky when one was on-call at night. These last bastions of psychotic chronicity were inhabited by patients who were difficult to place in more homely facilities in the community. Rosa was one of them.

She had been born in the 1920s in a very religious and yet very disorganised family. Her mother was mentally ill and her father had already left the family home by the time Rosa was born. Rosa's mother was disabled by her illness and unable to cope without support (or even with support, probably). She couldn't possibly care for Rosa or her older siblings, who were admitted to a children's institution.

I feel myself becoming increasingly sad as I write these lines about Rosa. Had she grown up in a stable, caring family, her childhood would hardly merit a mention here and my mind would not feel the need to tune up emotionally and sympathise with Rosa as a child and all her deprivations.

Rosa experienced a relatively brief period of independence in her early adulthood. I was going to write *"enjoyed"* a period of independence, but I don't think she did, unless one considers poverty and prostitution as things that can be enjoyed. Shortly after the war Rosa became ill, so ill in fact that she apparently reached a state of "stupor", mute, motionless and unresponsive. So she was institutionalised again, for the second and definitive time in her life. She never left hospital.

ECT brought her out of her stupor, it seems, but she remained constantly sad, distressed and very psychotic, a victim of horrendous depressive delusions. I'm not going to reflect here on whether she was so ill as a result of her awful life, or whether perhaps she, and her mother before her, had such awful lives because of their illnesses, or perhaps both. In any case, a decision was made at some point to try to stop her suffering by disconnecting some of the fibres that link the frontal lobe to the emotional centres of the brain. Following the operation,

Rosa became more placid and more settled generally, but also flatter in affect, with no initiative and no drive. She would apparently stay in the same corner of her room for the whole day, staring into space and perhaps picking her nose. Much of the distress had gone, along with the spark of her soul. She communicated less and less. Unfortunately, her psychosis never subsided completely.

Some years after I first met Rosa, I visited the same hospital to attend a presentation on a new and allegedly revolutionary drug (it wasn't revolutionary at all, actually, they hardly ever are) and I immediately got lost while looking for the main meeting room. Getting lost in hospitals is something I do frequently, even in those I am supposed to know well. Their disconcerting corridors feel like an allegory of the anxieties and uncertainties associated with the treatment of every human illness. I soon found myself in the old clinical part of the complex, with its towering high ceilings, enormous cast iron radiators and intricately tiled floors. Most of it seemed decommissioned and abandoned. As I passed by an open door leading to a large communal area, I saw several old patients sitting in front of a TV screen in a semicircle. One of them wasn't looking at the TV; she looked instead at the open door, where I was, with an enigmatic smile. It was Rosa.

I went into the room to say hello to her, but I don't think she recognised me. A severe looking male Asian nurse approached us.

"Are you a relative?" he asked, surprised to see that Rosa had a visitor.

"No, I used to work here. How is Rosa doing?"

"You know, if you had asked me that question at anytime in the last few years, I'd have answered 'she went mute at some point and now we don't know if she is really with us anymore or not'."

The nurse's face had softened while explaining Rosa's progress. He continued:

"And then, only the other day, she suddenly smiled, as she often does, and said 'happy'. Nothing more, only 'happy'. So you know, I want to believe she is happy."

So did I.

In Greek mythology, *Psyche* ("Breath", or "Soul") was a princess, often represented wearing the wings of a butterfly. *Cupid* ("Desire") and *Psyche* fell in love and had a daughter called *Hedone* ("Pleasure").

Our psyche isn't a mythological butterfly. It has instead a very authentic existence in the here and now. Emotions, as well as any other expressions of our psyche, are real, concrete events, felt by the brain, in the brain. They are the result of neuro-chemical phenomena, some of which can be reproduced artificially. It is difficult to see body and mind as separate entities when we know that every little change in one of them may have a significant impact on the other. For instance, factors such as a hormonal imbalance, a cancer, or an infection, can affect the mind directly, whereas a depressive illness can also affect the cardiovascular and immune systems.

The brain uses chemical messengers, called neurotransmitters, to connect one cell with another. As we noted at the beginning of the book, there are ten trillion of these connections. Let's explore some of these chemical messengers and structures individually.

Serotonin is involved with mood. It is the neurotransmitter that has been most closely associated with the idea of happiness, mainly because newer antidepressants, like Prozac for instance, are thought to improve depression by enhancing serotonin activity in the brain. However, serotonin does many other things. In fact, it isn't named after any happiness-inducing properties, but after the effect it has on the walls of blood vessels. About 90% of our serotonin resides in the gut, but it is also released by small clusters of cells in the brain stem and then projected on to the whole of the central nervous system. It modulates mood, but is also involved in learning, motivation, sleep and movement. If one overdoes the dose of an antidepressant of the Prozac family (those that primarily enhance Serotonin are called SSRIs), one may induce something called a Serotonin Syndrome, ironically characterised by symptoms that are pretty much the same as those that one is trying to treat, such as agitation and intense anxiety, only more extreme. This sometimes results in the doctor increasing the dose, believing the patient has become even more depressed, with awful consequences.

There is no proportional correlation between serotonin levels of activity in the brain and wellbeing, so it is clear that this chemical is not a panacea for happiness.

Feelings of reward are mediated through Dopamine. To put it very crudely, this is the messenger that is a little too active in schizophrenia and not active enough in Parkinson's disease. The buzz we feel when we hit the jackpot in the fruit machine is the result of certain areas of the brain being showered with dopamine. Because of this, this messenger is thought to be implicated in many types of addictive behaviour. There is something called "dopamine dysregulation syndrome", which is what happens sometimes to those who have taken dopaminergic medications for Parkinson's for a long time. Victims of this syndrome may develop a taste for gambling, excessive shopping, or become hyper-sexual. The fact that we need to subdue dopamine transmission in the brain in order to improve the symptoms of schizophrenia clearly shows that dopamine, like serotonin, isn't a panacea for happiness either, or even an advisable means of obtaining constant pleasure, as the famous experiment by James Olds and Peter Milner demonstrated in the 1950s. They implanted tiny electrodes into the brains of rats that delivered a small electric charge to the pleasure centres deep in the brain whenever the rat pushed a lever. They found that the rat would push the lever thousands of times, so gratified by this strange magical pleasure machine that it forgot to eat or drink and eventually died. If the rats were given a substance to block dopamine, they stopped pushing the lever, which proved that the rodent's pleasure had been facilitated by this neurotransmitter.

Noradrenaline is the chemical messenger that facilitates the "fight or flight" response. It concerns itself with acute threats and therefore has very little to do with happiness.

GABA (I won't bother the reader with the meaning of this acronym) modulates fear and over-arousal. It is essentially an inhibitory chemical that damps down the type of signal that noradrenaline is keen to emphasise, by hindering the alarm mechanisms in the brain. That's why those drugs that act on the GABA receptors, such as valium and xanax, which belong to a family called benzodiazepines, have such a nice, chilling effect.

The first benzodiazepine was developed in 1955 by a Polish chemist, called Leo Sternbach, who was working in New Jersey at the time. They called it librium. These drugs appeared to be very effective and safe, so they quickly became a huge commercial success. It is estimated that by the beginning of the 1980s, one in ten men and one in five women in Britain were consuming this type of tranquilliser. Then a realisation emerged that coming off valium was sometimes problematic and that benzodiazepines could be addictive. Prescriptions dropped hugely, swinging the pendulum from a devil-may-care, dishing-it-out liberal position, to the current puritanical "valium is nice and it's addictive, so it must surely be evil" perception. "Needing" the drug is thought to be an indicator of addiction, but some people need benzodiazepines for their anxiety in a way that is comparable to how a diabetic needs insulin, and yet we wouldn't say that the diabetic is "addicted" to the insulin.

It is worthwhile reflecting on the fact that when benzodiazepines were more freely available, a substantial chunk of the population received a prescription for them. Even more never reached the doctor's office and suffered in silence, as many still do. Anxiety is, unfortunately, extremely common. The simple reason for its ubiquity is that fear favours survival, which is the number one priority in our genetic code. The signal associated with it must inevitably be alarming and unpleasant. In fact, it needs to be impossible to ignore, like a baby crying, or a flame burning our skin. It can be argued that feeling a little frightened is in fact quite appropriate because being alive is a dangerous business. Even the luckiest person will have to face adversity and eventual death. Very inaccurately, a lack of fear has been equated with courage, when in fact courage consists in the ability to overcome fear, not in the inability to feel it.

Oxytocin is a curious chemical messenger. It has myriad functions, from the boringly physiological to the excitingly romantic. It was named after its obstetric properties (it facilitates the delivery of the baby), but it also has an interesting psychological role as the catalyst of social and romantic bonding. It is, in other words, the magic potion that makes us fall in love. By strengthening social bonding, oxytocin may also be implicated, allegedly, in promoting feelings of xenophobia against those outside that social bond, which isn't so romantic.

Incidentally, the time when we feel closest to happiness is when we fall in love, as long as it is reciprocated, of course. When it isn't, we may experience a "broken heart syndrome", or *Takotsubo's cardiomyopathy*, as it is known in medicine, which affects the muscle of the heart and can be life-threatening. Either way, as everybody knows and love songs constantly remind us, romantic love is the source of many intense and conflicting emotions that are unlikely to keep us happy for very long.

The brain, where all these substances – and many more in fact – go about their business, includes some structures that are evolutionarily very old and can even be found in reptiles. In fact, the brains of other vertebrates don't look that different from ours because they all share the same basic components. However, the evolutionary newer bits in our brain, such as the frontal part of the cortex, are more specific to humans and give us the intellectual powers unique to our species. There is a formation in the centre of the brain that is ancient and also particularly relevant here because this is where our emotional life resides.[7] An American neuroscientist called Paul MacLean, son of a Presbyterian minister, first described what he called the "limbic system", the border area *("limbus")* between the higher and newer surface of the brain itself and the lower structures at the base of this organ. It carries out the initial or preliminary processing of emotions and emotional responses and then sends this information up to structures above it in the brain cortex for final processing, in a two–tier administrative system, which seems a little bureaucratic, but highlights the fact that Nature has taken the neurological management of our emotions very seriously.

A crucial component of the limbic system is the *Hippocampus*, so called because it resembles a sea-horse in shape. It is intimately involved with the formation and storage

---

7 The presence of this "emotional brain" in other animals makes it very difficult (impossible in my view) to argue that they are not able to suffer, as we are, when they are being chased or mistreated.

of memories[8]. There are in fact two of them, located either side and deep into the brain, and connected with a variety of senses, which explains how an old memory can be suddenly evoked by a specific smell or a melody. A memory that has been retrieved in this way, after the emotional brain communicated with one of the senses, may carry a powerful emotional content.

Attached to the *Hippocampus*, we find two little globules that look like almonds. They are the right and left *Amygdala*, Theses little blobs are responsible for the emotional manifestation of our most terrifying inner demons because they play a crucial role in generating and modulating feelings of fear and anger. A heightened activation of the *Amygdala* has been found to be associated with all sorts of psychological disorders, particularly those that are to do with feeling afraid, like anxiety disorders and post-traumatic stress. Curiously, a study carried out by researchers at University College London, in which a group of young adults agreed to have their brains scanned in an MRI machine after confessing their political sympathies, found that greater political conservatism was associated with a larger *Amygdala*. Make of that what you will.

While pondering the role of the *Amygdala* in my way to a meeting, a minor road incident provides a useful but unwelcome illustration of its function. I first notice a vague feeling of apprehension creeping into my mind. This anxiety isn't focused on anything in particular necessarily, although it wouldn't take much searching to find a few potentially scary issues currently present in my life. I suppose I could label my anxiety as "free-floating", which is a very common type, although knowing

8 London black cab drivers have been shown to have a larger *Hippocampus* than the general public, possibly because they need to store vast amounts of visual information on the streets of London (and many political views) in their brains.

that it is an ordinary sort of anxiety doesn't make it any more bearable. I am then suddenly startled by another car coming very close to my tailgate, full beam on, honking its horn in long, aggressive dashes. I now feel acute anger and fright on top of the pre-existing free-floating apprehension. I can imagine my own *Amygdala* firing wildly and sending shrill electro-chemical messages to the upper strata of my brain, letting them know, first, of its indistinct fear that something frightening could happen (the foreboding feeling), followed by an urgent report that something frightening did happen after all (the threatening aggression from the stupid driver), and concluding with a sense of intense indignation and a pressing request for a violent retaliation against the perpetrator of this outrage (such as slowing down on purpose while aiming insulting gestures at the other driver and then challenging him to a race and/or a fist fracas by the roadside). The cerebral cortex, very maturely, rejects the request. I just let the idiot pass me. My *Amygdala* carries on firing for a long while after the incident.

The *Nucleus Accumbens* is another conglomeration of neurons that is considered to be part of the limbic system, placed, very roughly, between the *Amygdala* and the eyes. This nucleus concerns itself with pleasure and reward and is therefore the bit in the brain that is quite partial to all the agreeable vices of the flesh and the mind, and their associated addictions. As we have seen, pleasure and reward, which are the primary business of this nucleus, are largely mediated through dopamine. Unfortunately, the poor rats in the Olds and Milner's experiment demonstrated that Nature cannot allow pleasure to be permanent and sustained because it would otherwise interfere with the animal's survival mechanisms.

The emotional systems in the brain are complex and fragile and the emotions associated with them can be ephemeral and sometimes autonomous. We tend to believe that the whole of our psychological life is the result of whatever is happening to us, that our emotions are purely reactive to our environment and our life history. This is of course largely true, but also true is the fact that the brain does its own thing and may decide to fire or inhibit certain regions, connections and systems in an endogenous, arbitrary and relatively unpredictable manner. This has been called "mental weather". I find that a bad emotional day is a little more endurable when I think of it as a rainy day that will pass. Bad weather, that's all.

We have seen that the intricate circuitry of the brain and the chemical messengers that bring it alive have powerful ways of alarming and distressing us, and that the pleasurable, equivalent mechanisms, never seem to be quite so assertive, permanent or reliable. In fact, mental illness and unspecific psychological distress can be undistinguishable sometimes, except that the distress associated with the hardships of life is more immediately understandable. This supports the notion that mental illness expresses itself through perfectly natural, deeply ingrained, sturdy, and ready-made patterns of unhappiness.

Given that we know which parts of the brain are responsible for our anxieties and distress, it's not surprising that some doctors decided to take a surgical approach in the treatment of severe mental illness, by destroying or disconnecting the offending components. A Portuguese neurologist called Egas Moriz, who received a Nobel Prize for his work, pioneered psychosurgery in the 1930s (it had already been attempted unsuccessfully in the 19th century), but it was an American called Walter Freeman who really popularised the procedure in the 1950s. In his book on the history of psychiatry, the historian Edward Shorter explains how Freeman travelled the length of the United States in a station wagon car filled with his surgical paraphernalia and camping equipment, performing demonstrations in the cities he visited, like a snake oil salesman. Freeman was an example of 1950s American technological optimism in a 1950s American *on-the-road* setting. It was later in the same decade that the first antipsychotic drugs were developed and this crucial breakthrough reduced the demand for lobotomies to almost zero. Thousands of people had lobotomies performed, including Evita Perón, shortly before she died in 1952. She had developed problematic psychological symptoms secondary to her cancer, although the operation may have been performed to control the pain, or perhaps to control *her*, depending on which author you believe.

Rosa's lobotomy was the only means doctors had available at the time to curtail her constant suffering and tame the ugly punishment processes that had gone awry in her brain, like one of those rogue immune systems that turn against their owners in auto-immune diseases like Lupus or Crohn's. The difference between the immune and the limbic systems is that the latter makes us suffer even when it is functioning correctly.

I like to imagine Rosa's psyche as a beautiful mythological butterfly. But I fear that this particular butterfly was kidnapped by the repulsive demon of her untreatable mental illness.

CHAPTER 5

DRUGS AND HAPPY PILLS

To fall in Hell or soar angelic
You'll need a pinch of psychedelic

Humphry Fortescue Osmond,
British psychiatrist

Establishing clearly and without a doubt what medication an old patient is taking precisely at a given time is curiously difficult. It is as if a medication list was a fluid, relative notion, like an abstract concept, and not the hard fact that it is meant to be. Compiling this long list during a consultation with an older patient, in the middle of a busy clinic, can be a stressful task.

"So I see in your repeat prescription from the surgery that you take: *amlodipine, clopidogrel, lansoprazole, digoxin, sodium valproate, buscopan, codeine phosphate, atorvastatin, furosemide, multivitamins, sitagliptin, amiodarone, isosorbide, tamsulosin, ferrous sulphate, calcium, allopurinol, glucosamine, docusate sodium, irbesartan*, and of course the antidepressant I prescribed for you, *mirtazapine*."

"Yes, I've been on them pills for a long time, but I'm not taking the last one".

She replies confidently, and I see in her face that she can't wait to tell me why.

"Which one?"

"The antidepressant. *Mirtazapine* I think it's called"

"And why is that?"

Here comes the anticipated explanation.

"I'm not much of a pill person, you know. I never liked taking tablets".

The probable real reason why Maureen isn't taking the antidepressant I prescribed for her depression, and also to help her sleep at night (which has recently been a major problem for her), is that she, like many others, relates to psychotropic drugs differently to how she relates to the awfully long list of regular pills that she takes for her physical health. It isn't a fear of side-effects, which of course psychiatric drugs do have; otherwise she wouldn't be prepared to take the other pills either. It is instead a vague apprehension of changing, of becoming a different Maureen, one that has been mutated by an artificial chemical substance.

I see Maureen again in clinic two months later. She didn't attend her last appointment with me a week ago. Her care coordinator, with whom she gets on very well, informs me that she remains depressed and anxious. She is not really functioning very well at all and her two daughters are worried.

"Awful, doctor, Never in all my years I've felt this bad. One mustn't grumble, though."

This is Maureen's reply when I ask her how she is doing. Older patients frequently say they shouldn't grumble, unlike the younger ones, who do grumble a lot, but often with very good reasons, one has to admit.

"So how come we didn't see you in the clinic a week ago?"

"Sorry doctor, I couldn't come; I had a doctor's appointment."

Psychiatrists like to see themselves as proper medical doctors. We are doctors of the mind, but the relative woolliness of our discipline devalues our status within the medical profession and patients like Maureen sometimes prioritise the care they receive from specialists who look after other parts of their bodies.

Many of us believe that what philosophers call the "Cartesian" divide between body and mind is in fact artificial and invalid. This "Cartesian dualism", which sounds a bit daunting, simply refers to the theory, postulated by the French philosopher René Descartes, that body and mind are fundamentally different things and belong in separate realms. It's interesting to note that some of Descartes' philosophical insights came to him in the form of a revelation within a dream, like a sort of mystical experience. It has been argued, by the way, that at least one of the famous successive revelatory dreams he had on the night of November 10, 1619, when he was woken by a loud noise in his head and a bright flash of light, may have been in fact a manifestation of an "exploding head syndrome". It may sound unlikely, but this is a very real syndrome, in which the sufferer does hear a very loud noise in their head when falling asleep or waking up, as if it was exploding. It's unsettling, but not serious.

Knowing what we know about the physiological workings of the brain, we can disagree with Descartes and assert that emotions and moods, whether pleasant or unpleasant, are not mere abstractions that float in an ill-defined, ethereal spirit. The mind is indeed abstract, but only as the manifestation, or projection, of the physical brain.

Cutting brain connections surgically and irreversibly, as in Rosa's case, carried very substantial risks, chief among them the very high probability of inducing a "frontal lobe syndrome".

It would have been more accurate to call it a "*no* frontal lobe syndrome", as this clinical picture of disinhibition, shallow affect and loss of interest in one's surroundings is in fact what happens when the frontal lobe ceases to function properly.

The first (and perhaps most famous) reported case of frontal lobe syndrome was that of Phineas Gage, a 19th century American railroad foreman, who had a work accident involving explosives, in which a one metre (three feet) long iron rod shot through his cheekbone, crossed his head, and landed 25 metres (over 80 feet) away, The rod completely destroyed his left (dominant) frontal lobe. According to contemporary accounts, Phineas's character changed dramatically, from his usual dependable and considerate personality, to the foolish and dissolute man he became after the metal rod took away part of the person he had been. Rosa didn't become dissolute or foolish, but the lobotomy did flatten and dull her spirit.

When the opportunity arose in the 1950s to influence the workings of the brain by reversible chemical means (rather than surgical), psychiatrists jumped at it. This was nothing short of a revolution at the time, but very little has happened since. The drugs we use nowadays aren't much better than the ones invented 60 years ago, with a few notable exceptions.

We must make something very clear straight away: psychiatric drugs are not meant to make anybody feel happy, and this includes antidepressants. They wouldn't know how, or where, to exert a hypothetical happiness action. We have considered locations in the brain that make us suffer or feel pleasure, but there isn't a happiness centre to be found, either in the limbic system or in the evolutionary newer cerebral cortex that sits on top of it. There isn't such a thing as a happiness neurotransmitter either, as we have seen. Not even serotonin. And however hard we look for such nuclei and such neurotransmitters, they will never be found, I believe, simply because happiness is an abstract philosophical idea that cannot be transplanted into the neural machinery of our central nervous system.

Maureen, and many others, fears that if she takes an antidepressant when her mood is low, any potential gains in terms of wellbeing attributable to the tablet will be achieved illicitly and will therefore be fake and even *wrong*. In his influential book *"Listening to Prozac"*, Peter Kramer notes that people find it difficult to trust antidepressants because they think that a drug that makes them happy must be morally bad. An American psychiatrist called Gerald L. Klerman very aptly termed this attitude as *"pharmacological Calvinism"*. In an article published in 1972, he carried this religious metaphor, stating: *"abstinence [from any drugs] is the highest ideal, the purest route to pharmacological salvation"*.

In reality, antidepressants not only lack the ability to make anybody *happy*, they aren't even that good necessarily at treating depression. Don't get me wrong, they do work in some instances and I do prescribe them when I think they might help, but a review study published in the British Medical Journal concluded some years ago that SSRI antidepressants (the most commonly prescribed drugs of this type) *"do not have a clinically meaningful advantage over placebo"* (sugar pills). They may also have side-effects, of course, such as blunting of the libido, which seems paradoxical, considering that they are supposed to promote feelings of psychological wellbeing. This is in fact one of the most frequently cited reasons for stopping antidepressants. Other psychotropic drugs generally fare better. Antipsychotics improve psychosis, tranquillisers tranquillise, and mood stabilisers are good at stabilising mood. They all reduce suffering and help take away the awful pain of mental illness, which is no small feat. But none of them make us happy. At best, they bring us back to baseline.

How about Recreational Drugs?

Alexander Fleming, the discoverer of penicillin, said that *"penicillin cures, but wine makes people happy"*. Bringing ephemeral joy is what recreational drugs do.

Trainspotting, the 1996 black comedy film directed by Danny Boyle, had street drug addiction as one of its main themes. It was criticised by some because the film showed the protagonists having great fun while taking drugs. It is clear however that people take recreational drugs because they find the experience enjoyable; otherwise they wouldn't do it. Evidently however, the drug taking is unlikely to result in a long term net gain in terms of enjoyment, once all the risks and drawbacks have been taken into account. Others take drugs or alcohol not to have great fun necessarily, but to self-medicate their psychological pain.

Lately, an interesting overlap between medicinal and street drugs is finally being recognised. Ketamine, for instance, is a drug used in medicine for a variety of purposes and is also appreciated in the streets as a very powerful tranquilliser. In recent times, it has also been shown to be strikingly effective in the treatment of some depressions. Depressed patients who failed to respond to multiple interventions sometimes improve in a matter of minutes after receiving an intravenous infusion of ketamine. A "dissociative reaction", such as an "out of body experience", in which the patient sees herself from outside her own body, is a relatively common adverse, but arguably interesting, reaction.

Psychedelic drugs, such as Psilocybin (magic mushrooms), or Mescaline, are being researched as possible agents for the treatment of depression and anxiety. The very word *"psychedelic"* means "psyche-uncovering", or "soul-manifesting". They received this name because these substances were thought to facilitate access to one's very soul. Native Americans, both in the North and in the South of the continent, used psychedelics for this purpose in their religious ceremonies.

Humphry Osmond was a British psychiatrist who became very interested in mescaline in the nineteen-fifties, a very lively and open-minded decade as far as searching for novel mental health treatments was concerned. I realise that "1950s" and "open-minded" don't necessarily go together very well, but in comparison we now seem to lack the degree of technological optimism and intellectual curiosity that characterised mental health research during that period. Of course, this research was not always conducted in a way that we would find acceptable nowadays.

Osmond thought that psychedelics opened a window into the mysteries of psychosis. He met and corresponded with Aldous Huxley, the celebrated author, and actually provided some mescaline for him. The ensuing result was a book called *The Doors of Perception*, in which Huxley described in very mystical terms his psychedelic experience. Despite this spike of interest about 70 years ago, psychedelic drugs have remained confined, until very recently, to the underground world of illegal narcotics.

We have been aware for centuries that these drugs have very obvious mind-altering properties, and yet we seem to be curiously reluctant to explore their possible therapeutic value in the treatment of psychological suffering. It is as if we couldn't possibly come to terms with the possibility of curing sadness with the help of a potentially pleasurable intervention. We seem to be stuck in a mind frame in which a benefit in health can only be purchased through sacrifice and pain, as we shall see in the next chapter.

Leaving medicinal possibilities aside, the main problem with recreational drugs, other than the risks they may pose, is that the chemical short-cut to pleasure that they offer is crude and not always reliable. If they could be trusted to transport us to a good place every time we took them, we would have a panacea to pleasure, which would transform our world radically.

Brave New World

Aldous Huxley himself had described such a "new world", a *Brave New World*, as he called his novel, about 20 years before he experimented with mescaline. The inhabitants of this curious story lived perfectly happy lives with the help of *soma*, the state-provided drug that kept them docile but content. Everybody is happy (in a way) in Huxley's world. Not bad for a dystopia.

The idea of a dull and flat placidity being extended to a whole society turns up in a number of fictional dystopias. They are the equivalent of mass lobotomies, imposed on the people by chemicals, cerebral implants, or perhaps through a particularly effective modality of sustained propaganda, as a way of perpetuating power and ensuring obedience. Is this monotonous contentment, this freedom from wanting and anxiety, an inferior type of happiness?

"Life at its noblest leaves mere happiness far behind; and indeed cannot endure it", said George Bernard Shaw. The idea behind this statement is that being human is about embracing conflict and adversity, which is obviously at odds with a state of continuous and unruffled tranquillity. We are assuming here that an artificial pseudo-happiness must be necessarily flat and stale. We have in fact seen that there is no such a thing as a "happiness centre" in the brain that could be switched on synthetically, but we can still consider the possibility, *theoretically* at least, that one day it might be possible to induce a state of real and unremitting

bliss, which would even contain Maslow's "peak experience" feelings, by means of some amazing technological intervention that we cannot even start to imagine at the moment. Would this heaven still be inferior to a conflicted and painful, albeit authentic, human existence?

Robert Nozick was an American psychologist who in 1974 proposed the idea of an "experience machine". He asked us to suppose that "superduper neuropsychologists" (as he called them) had figured out how to stimulate our brain through carefully placed hi-tech electrodes, in such a way that we would have all the lovely pleasure and contentment that we feel when life is going well, but importantly, we wouldn't even be aware of the fact that these lovely feelings had been artificially induced while we were under the influence of the machine. Would we choose to attach our brain to the "experience machine"? Nozick thought we wouldn't, because we value life as a real thing, not as a mere vehicle towards pleasure and happiness. I'm not so sure.

This is a purely philosophical question at the moment, as we simply lack, and probably always will lack, the technology to create artificial happiness, and even if we somehow did acquire such technology, Olds and Milner's rats showed that an unchallenged access to uninterrupted ecstasy would kill us all in no time at all. Like their rats, we would soon abandon all life-sustaining activities and devote ourselves exclusively to pressing the joy lever.

We have no pleasure lever, no "experience machine", and no *soma* at our disposal. Instead, we constantly have to put up with the many unpleasant bits that infect our existence. We have no choice on the matter, so we may as well cherish all this unpleasantness, the conflict and the sorrow, as the shadows that define our human world, the darkness that allows us to appreciate the light, and all that. But if we could somehow be happy, by any means, it would soon become very clear that suffering isn't morally or philosophically more elevated than joy, and that we couldn't be bothered with shadows if we could have instead all the light, all the time.

Technically, I should have discharged Maureen from my clinic at the last review. She wasn't willing to take psychiatric medication, didn't always attend her appointments, and she wasn't very severely depressed. But she is vulnerable and relatively isolated, so I decided to see her again a couple of months later, just to make sure she is still stable.

Today, she comes to the clinic early and sits in the waiting area impatiently. When she finally enters the consulting room, she is obviously downcast and even a little tremulous. It is obvious she has been crying because her brown eyes, always disproportionally large in her small face, are a little red.

"I know you can't help me," she starts, after a few seconds of initial silence. "You know I had been feeling low and very lonely, my daughter never seems to want to spend any time with me, and I also told you, I think, that they found a lump in my breast, and then..."

Maureen breaks down at this point and starts crying, her big brown eyes wet with copious tears and contracted in anguish.

"Yesterday I was driving home" (she still drives, despite the many ailments both she and her ancient Rover have) "and I couldn't believe how lucky I was with the lights, they were all green the whole way. The moment I arrived home, the telephone rang. It was Janet. She had been my closest friend for many years, but then she moved to Scotland and we couldn't keep in touch as often as before, and then, one day she told me she got cancer in her womb. Anyway, Janet is –was- my soulmate, more so than my late husband. We grew up together; we were inseparable, me and Janet."

Maureen stops again and clasps her face in her hands, unable to contain her tears.

"Janet was calling me from Dignitas in Switzerland. She wanted to speak to me before she had the injection. She wanted me to be the last person she spoke to on Earth. If the traffic lights hadn't been all green, I would have missed the call. I can't think of anything else since she called. Janet dying, my dear Janet, that's all I can think about".

Maureen is right. All the antidepressants in the world wouldn't take her pain away, even if her grief had the bitter-sweet taste of an enormously moving goodbye after a lifetime of friendship. And Maureen wouldn't take them anyway.

Others aren't like Maureen and believe that our pills will be able to soothe the throbbing in their souls like a paracetamol calms a headache, even if their souls are hurting because of an awful loss, or an illness[9], or because they are stuck with an unloving spouse. Pills can sometimes take the edge out of the suffering, but unfortunately they don't do much more than this in such situations.

When the British Medical Journal ran a vote amongst its readers back in 2002, asking them to identify the "top 10 non-diseases", unhappiness was included in the list, together with other pseudo-illnesses, such as baldness, pregnancy, boredom, or being ugly. This is perhaps a little unkind. Unhappiness is not a medical disorder, as we shall see at the end of the book, but it is a sort of disease; one that affects us all, at least much of the time, and can't be cured with pills or with a scalpel.

---

[9] Physical and psychological pain coexist so frequently and relate to each other in such complex ways that it could be argued that emotional pain is *actual pain* and not a mere metaphor of its physical equivalent.

CHAPTER 6

FOOD AND SEX

"How are you getting on with the pills I gave you? Any side-effects?"

I ask Laszlo, a very charming and polite Hungarian unemployed solicitor in his early forties. His case is particularly challenging because he has a bipolar disorder, as well as traits of Asperger's syndrome. In other words, he is very incompetent socially (he is "on the spectrum", as some say), as well as having a very labile mood. I gave him an antiepileptic drug that acts as a mood stabiliser and should help modulate his ups and downs, of which he has many.

"No problem, the pills are OK." I notice a slight hesitation in his reply. "The only thing is, I wonder if they may be affecting my libido. Over the last few days I've had an average amount of sex, twice with a woman and another time with a guy..."

"Well", I interrupt, "doesn't sound as if there is much wrong with your libido!"

In a different bipolar patient, having sex with strangers might indicate that they are going a little "high" and disinhibited, but not necessarily in Lazlo's case, as we will explain.

"That may be so. But I didn't *enjoy it* that much."

He concludes in a quiet, conspiratorial voice.

Laszlo is a proper sexual hedonist, a dedicated and committed sexual athlete, for whom a tally of two or three sexual partners of both genders in a week isn't out of the norm. Despite his social awkwardness, he projects a paradoxical and difficult to define suave charm. He is tall, handsome and has piercing green eyes. For reasons that remain a little obscure, he is also well-off, even though he has only worked for short periods of time. It isn't surprising therefore that he has no difficulty finding willing partners, but I never explored this in great detail because, to be frank, I find his sexual escapades a little sordid. They are clearly not too sordid for him and even during the dark and wintry depths of his regular periods of depression Laszlo is able to find some solace in sex. The only difference is that when he is not feeling very well, he doesn't enjoy it very much. And he is depressed now.

Some depressions are characterised by fear, others mainly by regret, or fatigue, or even despair. Laszlo's is defined by a painfully impaired ability to experience pleasure, which he sees as his *raison d'être*.

A depressed state is devoid of pleasure. *"How weary, stale, flat, and unprofitable seem to me all the uses of this world!"* says a clearly depressed Hamlet, whereas happiness, when we do experience it, is able to find pleasure in the small joys of daily existence. These joys are so small and so many (smell of coffee, gloves fitting snugly, car accelerating smoothly, sitting on a soft sofa) that they could be termed the "plankton" or "dark matter" of pleasure. Life would be unbearable without this plankton of tiny gratifying firings in our brain tissue. There is therefore a clear connection between pleasure and happiness. In fact, Muslim physicians in the Middle Ages argued that the best way to cure melancholia was through hedonistic therapies, such as good food, baths, pleasant company, music and a little sex now and then. The Christian alternatives at the time were blood-letting and purges. I know which approach most melancholics would choose.

According to Augustine, the desire Adam felt in the Garden of Eden turned all his descendants into a *massa damnata* (a condemned mass) and the moral perils of desire have been present in the Christian conscience ever since. Pope Gregory I, the one credited with inventing Gregorian chant, is a good example of Christianity's traditional attitude to pleasure. He was born into a well-to-do Roman family in the 6th century but his approach to food was certainly different to that of modern Italians. He identified several different modalities of gluttony, in which the common factor was the *desire* for the food. He taught that one could sin by eating between meals (still a dietary sin to this day), eating fancy foods, eating too much, or just by being too much of a foodie in general. He also illustrated the awful sinfulness of culinary lust with episodes of various biblical characters being justly punished by God with death after indulging in a spot of superfluous brunch, or because they cooked their lamb in a different way to how honest folk had always prepared it, which must be, I suppose, one of the earliest records in gastronomic experimentation.

We still moralise our food, like we do with all other pleasures. To put it simply, greens and fibre we see as good, whereas fats and carbohydrates are evil.

Simultaneously, we are witnessing a growing trend towards the demonisation of sugar, with calls for a tax on sugary drinks.

Product information in the supermarket shelves often includes moral claims, with labels such as "fair trade", "be good to yourself", or "drink responsively".

The empirical evidence supporting the health benefits of drinking alcohol in moderation was largely ignored by the British Chief Medical Officer, when she cut down the recommended daily limit in 2016. The press later revealed that the committee that drafted the guidelines had close links with the Temperance movement.

A preoccupation with eating "good" food can become so intense that it may eventually develop into a clinical syndrome called "orthorexia nervosa". Orthorexic patients apply moral qualities to their diet, developing in the process an affinity towards foods that are thought to improve health and strong – even pathological – aversions against those foods that are believed to damage it. The emotions involved are so strong that patients will sometimes paradoxically compromise their nutrition in their quest for the perfect diet.

The common factor in the preceding paragraphs is the moral dimension in our groceries and the effect of those moral qualities on our health. But applying a human moral construct to Nature by dividing foods and lifestyles into good and bad is misleading. In reality, nothing in Nature is either good or bad in itself. For instance, our bodies need cholesterol for a variety of important purposes, while exercise, on the other hand, can be potentially dangerous and therefore capable of ending our lives prematurely.

We tend to attribute moral characteristics to food and lifestyle choices according to a perceived inverse correlation between pleasure and health. In this perverse "pleasure economy", life can only be extended by renouncing and containing hedonism, just like the virtuous renounced all the dissipations of the flesh in order to access paradise in more religious times than ours. In this way, a wholesome and unpleasurable diet, in conjunction with daily, and equally unpleasurable and strenuous exercise, will earn us the right to prolong our lives, while indulging in unearned and therefore illicit pleasure (such as alcohol, fats and sugar) will be punished with an early death.

In fact, Nature is only concerned with survival and reproduction, as we saw in the chapter on evolution. Indeed, we like fats and sugar precisely because the scarcity of high calorie nutrition was the main threat to survival in pre-industrial societies. In the Middle Ages, our ancestors died when the crops failed and would have jumped at the chance of acquiring obesity-induced diabetes as an alternative to their hunger. So it is Nature that has programmed us to desire calories, for the same reason it programmed us to like sex: having a desire for fats and sex helps with survival and reproduction. Good things are associated with pleasure precisely because they are good for us, while we associate bad and dangerous things with fear and pain. "Nothing would be more tiresome than eating and drinking if God had not made them a pleasure as well as a necessity", said Voltaire.

Unfortunately, pleasure can also be problematic for survival when it can be experienced without any constraints or limits. When pleasure can be had constantly, the benefit that was originally associated with it and facilitated survival – in this case, the energy contained in fats and sugar – is cancelled.

Just as we feel the need to tame our sexual desires with moral rules in order to avoid social chaos, we also seem to have developed the need to moralise other pleasurable choices, now that our access to them has become too easy.

Ultimately, Nature does not really care much about our moral choices. Even the nutritionally- virtuous will inevitably die one day, just like the rest of us, and perhaps not much later. But even if you overcome the moral barrier that Pope Gregory erected between you and your culinary naughty pleasures, abandoning yourself to gluttony still won't make you happy.

As if moral obstacles weren't enough to separate us from an enjoyable existence, the so-called "Paradox of Hedonism" makes even the pursuit of pleasure itself tricky. Pleasure, it seems, cannot be obtained directly, so the paradox is that the more one seeks it, the more that seeking gets in the way of acquiring it. Pleasure, some say, can only happen as a by-product of other activities, such as altruism, or otherwise by accident, when one least expects it. Pleasure needs to surprise you. If it is announced in advance of its expected arrival, it seems to lose much of its fizziness and vibrancy in the process.

Undoubtedly, there is some truth in the Paradox of Hedonism, but it is also obvious, in my view, that pleasure can be obtained directly and very frequently (ask any cigarette smoker), if one doesn't mind much about staying at the hedonistic level and not progressing towards a more satisfying and profound state of happiness, which, this book argues, is the truly elusive goal.

In the mind of John Stuart Mill, the 19th century British philosopher and liberal politician, happiness was "intended pleasure, and the absence of pain" while he saw unhappiness as "pain, and the privation of pleasure". This is neat and logical in an almost arithmetical and mechanical kind of way. Mill postulated that happiness is the ultimate aim of all our desires. All we want is happiness, according to this philosophy, even when we think we want something else. "Happiness is the sole end of human action", he declared.

Mill was ahead of his time in many respects. After enduring a particularly severe upbringing under the direction of his dictatorial father, as well as a melancholic episode that brought him to the brink of suicide at the age of 20, he became a distinguished thinker and, in his role as MP for Westminster, a political champion of very modern causes, such as women's suffrage and the protection of the environment. On the other hand, he also defended the empire by arguing that the civilised colonisers were superior to the indigenous colonised, which goes to prove that no-one is perfect.

Mill wasn't the first English philosopher to ponder these issues. Almost one century before him, Jeremy Bentham founded a philosophical approach to happiness based on the "utility" of those things that give us pleasure, which came to be called "utilitarianism". Bentham was certainly an unusual character. You can still see him on the ground floor of UCL's Student Centre in London, sitting comfortably on a chair, inside a glass case. UCL's website explains that "the cabinet contains Bentham's preserved skeleton, dressed in his own clothes, and surmounted by a wax head". He believed that displaying himself (what he termed "auto-icon") would be more effective than a portrait, because "identity [is] preferable to similitude". His actual head, which turned out looking a little creepy after a less than perfect process of mummification, is kept separately inside a box. Bentham was as a proper utilitarian and therefore not too fussy about the quality of a given gratification, as long as it was enjoyable, whereas Mill thought that there was a hierarchy of pleasure, which has been a recurring theme over the centuries. In this "class system" of hedonism, the dissipations associated with the senses ("the works of the flesh", as the Bible would call them) were placed at the lower level, while things like altruism, philanthropy and the arts induce a more elevated, and therefore more desirable, type of joy, according to Mill. He also distinguished between the mere satisfaction of desire and a loftier and more ethereal happiness: "it is better to be a human being dissatisfied than a pig satisfied", he declared.

Like JS Mill, Sigmund Freud believed that humans are driven by a need to obtain pleasure and avoid pain. He called this the "pleasure principle". In psychoanalysis, the demands placed by the *"Id"* (the bottom layer in our psyche) to obtain immediate gratification are modulated and restrained by the "reality principle", which reminds us that the urge to pass wind very pleasurably and noisily during a meeting at work will unfortunately have to be deferred until a more appropriate time. Out of the three hierarchical sections of the psyche, it is the lowly *Id* that plays the silly farty part, and, being basic and instinctual, it needs to be governed by the more sensible and grown-up psychological strata (*ego* and *super-ego*), placed above it.

Long before Mill and Freud, the ancient world had already considered the merits of pleasure. The Greek philosopher Epicurus is forever associated with voluptuous and decadent carnality. Because of this, he has had an awfully bad press over the centuries, even though he was apparently a very decent chap. He was enormously famous in his time, but the emphasis he placed on leading a pleasant and pleasurable life was at odds with the very manly and stoical Roman and Christian cultures that followed this period of humanist enlightenment, relegating his legacy to a mere caricature, that of the debauched and dissolute drunkard and glutton. He has been described as the "proprietor of the kitchen, the tavern, and the brothel". And yet, far from being the amoral pig this caricature depicts, Epicurus valued simple pleasures enjoyed in moderation and actually taught his pupils that one should lead a moral life. They should do so not in fear of retribution from the gods, who according to Epicurus weren't that bothered about humans anyway, but because being good was more pleasant than being bad, which is very persuasive argument. However, so much talk of apparent wantonness and pleasantness, together with the fact that Epicurus didn't believe humans had an immortal soul, earned him a place in Dante's *Inferno*, specifically in the Sixth Circle of Hell, where he and his pupils were eternally kept inside burning coffins as a symbolic and ironic, if slightly harsh, punishment for having believed in life that their souls would die with them.

The ancient Greek inhabitants of Sybaris, in what is now Calabria in Southern Italy, were also known for their hedonistic inclinations. The Romans credited the sybarites with the invention of the chamber pot, a very modern convenience that exemplified the luxuriousness of sybarite life. In the end however, they were expelled from their land by other tribes, which ancient historians thought was a just reckoning for a life of excess and indulgence. Sodom, the morally questionable city in the Book of Genesis, had a comparable fate for comparable reasons, although the names of the inhabitants of Sodom and those of Sybaris have come to mean very different things in modern language.

We moralise food and we moralise sex because pleasure is a deeply moral concept. We see it as ephemeral, selfish and shallow, and therefore reprehensible morally. But in the final analysis, the moral barriers to pleasure are of relatively little importance. The very enjoyable medieval Muslim cure for melancholia was undoubtedly much more effective than the Christian bowel purges equivalent, but, in any case, the main relationship between pleasure and happiness operates in the opposite direction of causality: it is happiness that facilitates pleasure, not the other way around. Once you have somehow managed to be happy, you will enjoy not only cigarettes, food and sex, but life itself, even at its most dreary. You will, in a sentence, enjoy rainy Monday mornings.

Laszlo, unburdened either by moral scruples or by any hedonistic paradoxes, made increasingly desperate attempts to find psychological comfort in sexual excess, but this didn't help much. This particular depressive swing had become much worse than any he had suffered before. He was very depressed and becoming increasingly desperate, despite a series of changes in his medication and ongoing therapy. He even confessed that he didn't see much point in going on and had thought of ways of putting an end to it all. I then suggested ECT.

The ECT room is light and airy. It looks and feels like a small operating theatre, perhaps an endoscopy room. In fact, some years ago the same room in the hospital was used for endoscopy and for ECT on different days of the week, although this wasn't ideal. There are a few machines on trolleys, as you would expect in any theatre. One of them is the ECT machine itself. The atmosphere is quite relaxed and tranquil, compared to other hospital psychiatric settings. The anaesthetist, her assistant, a psychiatric nurse and myself populate the room and welcome Laszlo when he enters, accompanied by his care coordinator. He is our first patient today. Before they came into the room, we had gone through the morning list, pointing out any possible problems, and then we discussed politics and traffic problems for a little while. ECT is the most effective treatment there is in cases of deep and severe melancholia.

Laszlo is put to sleep with a very short-acting drug injected into his vein, followed by a muscle relaxant, which inhibits most of the motor component (that is, the observable seizure) of the epileptic fit induced by the small electric charge. I apply the electrodes to his temples and the energy is delivered, accompanied by a buzzing noise. Laszlo's toes and hands tremble for about 15 seconds and then they stop, very undramatically. He didn't feel a thing. Laszlo wakes up a few minutes later and has a cup of tea, still a little drowsy. The procedure is repeated twice a week for a period of six weeks.

"I'm all right, thanks."

This is Laszlo's reply, in his slightly high-pitch but well-modulated voice, when we meet again in the consulting room after the course of ECT. He is not psychologically minded and finds it difficult to describe emotions, so his response is a little laconic when I ask him how he is feeling. I have to rely on my objective observations, which suggest a vast improvement. He is not agitated anymore and his affect is bright and once again pleasant. He is his normal self again, the Laszlo between episodes. His care coordinator, a very sweet middle-aged

Nigerian woman, who is also in the room with us, confirms his improvement.

"The best thing, doctor," he tells me, "is that I am enjoying things again."

I know what he is referring to, but I'd rather not hear the details.

Unfortunately, Laszlo remained unstable and suffered two further episodes – a mania followed by a depression – in the year following the first course of ECT, but we found ways to control them a little better. The combination of his social disability and his very brittle mood made it too difficult for him to reach the levels of confidence and stability one would usually need to build a normal life. But with help and support, he was able to create a version of normality that worked relatively well.

He needed another course of ECT to bring him out of this latest episode of depression. Afterwards, we met in clinic again.

"You know the film *Love Actually*?" Laszlo asks out of the blue. "You know the guy in it that goes to America to find girls? I've decided to do the same, to go to America. My problem is England, it stifles me. I'll feel better in America."

My heart sinks.

"No, don't, Laszlo!"

I stop him firmly, weary of the obvious risks involved in such an outlandish plan. An unpleasant aspect of being a psychiatrist is the occasional need to tell people what they should and shouldn't do, reinforcing the perception that psychiatrists are essentially bossy and authoritarian.

"That movie is a romantic comedy, real life isn't like that, and in any case, the point of the film is that everyone needs love, you know, something stable."

"I know what I like, doctor, everyone talks about love and happiness, but I'm not sure what they mean. They are just cloudy, woolly words to me. What I like is physical contact, I like the fact that sex is tangible, it's real, and it makes me feels good. At least it does when I'm not ill."

I argued in vain that he was, by any standards, getting more than enough sex here in England and that he had no need to go to the US to find even more there. I also argued that he would find immigration problems and be very lonely in the US, but Laszlo didn't want his belief in his American erotic Shangri-La to be challenged.

He did go soon after. He sent me a postcard from Boston (I don't know why he chose Boston) and I never heard from him again. I would like to believe that he did make it after all, that he found a sensual path to personal completeness in the New World, but I know that's not true.

Laszlo was handicapped by his illness, unable to relate to others in a normal way because of his Asperger's syndrome, or to manage his life successfully because of the instability of his bipolar disorder. Incapable of transcending himself, of being with another in any significant sense, or to plan his future, his refuge was pleasure in the here and now. But he could only access this refuge between episodes. When he was manic, the predominant features were irritability and a sense of dysphoric, impatient urgency. When depressed, a heavy sadness crushed his soul like a black emotion made of iron.

We moralise and limit our access to the sensual gratification to be found in sex and food, and to make matters worse, the Paradox of Hedonism is an obstacle to the acquisition of such gratification. These would be major difficulties if hedonism was the preliminary step in a journey towards happiness, but this is not the case. As we have seen, pleasure doesn't give you happiness; it is the other way around.

The psychological wellbeing afforded by the ECT gave Laszlo back his sexual pleasure. Like other humans, Laszlo wasn't happy, but he couldn't even understand the concept, let alone experience it. Unlike many other humans, he was a master at managing and consuming pleasure, but only when he was feeling well. He wouldn't have used the word, but could only enjoy pleasure when he was feeling happy.

CHAPTER 7

WEALTH DOES MAKE YOU HAPPY AFTER ALL (TO A POINT)

Like the Irishman in the joke who is asked for directions to go to Cork and responds that if he wanted to go to Cork he wouldn't start from here, our quest for happiness starts from the wrong place, one in which need and want are all too often the prevailing themes.

George Bernard Shaw, who had a lot to say on happiness, declared: "*The man with a toothache thinks everyone happy whose teeth are sound. The poverty-stricken man makes the same mistake about the rich man.*" The poor man may or may not be right about the rich man, but there is no doubt that being poor does make any measure of happiness even harder to reach.

The satisfaction of basic material and biological needs is the main and most obvious obstacle that a large proportion of humanity encounters on a daily basis in their ambition to be happy. Poverty and illness too often stand in the way. To make matters worse, being poor will also increase the likelihood of being ill, reducing both life expectancy and quality of life. Poor health and no money will make a human life *"[...] nasty, brutish and short"*, to quote Thomas Hobbes, the 17th century English philosopher. He was referring to a world with no "social contract" when he coined that expression, which is what we find in failed states maligned by chronic poverty.

Looking at epidemiological and socio-demographic data, it soon becomes clear that bad stuff tends to cluster together:

not just poverty and illness, but also crime, ignorance, violence, obesity, extreme politics, prostitution, abuse, drugs, and just about any other bad thing you may care to mention. All these factors influence and perpetuate each other, but if poverty is taken out of the equation, then all the other elements improve, as if by magic.

We all know how important money is in our lives, but it is a social taboo to declare it openly. In fact, what we do say quite often is precisely the opposite: that money can't bring you happiness and all important things in life are free. We are brought up with the conflicting messages that we need to do well for ourselves and secure a good steady income in adult life, while on the other hand we are constantly reminded that materialism is the mother of all evils.

There is in fact a clear association between income and happiness, although this is not a linear correlation. As income increases, so do personal levels of wellbeing, but only to a certain extent, beyond which happiness reaches a stable plateau, regardless of any additional growth in income. This doesn't seem to apply to the very rich, who continue to derive pleasure from accumulating wealth, as we'll see below.

The so-called "Easterlin paradox", named after a Californian professor of economics, refers to the fact that our levels of happiness appear to have remained constant over time despite large and steady rises in wealth in the recent history of developed countries. The fact that wealth is not the only contributor to a sense of general satisfaction in life helps explain this paradox, of course, but so does the fact that the way we perceive our wealth is relative to that of others, and to our own income in the past. If everyone in our neighbourhood has an expensive German car and holidays in the South of France, then our own otherwise lovely holiday in Clacton-on-Sea and perfectly good second hand Korean car will feel a little insufficient. Conversely, being the only guy in the street with a colour TV in the early Seventies would have filled its owner with uncontainable pride.

Money doesn't buy happiness. But it does buy an awful lot of proxies to happiness, like better housing, health and education, a richer cultural life, leisure time, comfort in old age, and perhaps most important of all, it buys the privilege of not having to worry about money. None of these things amount to happiness, not even when they are grouped together, but their absence inevitably brings substantial misery. In short, money makes us happy, but only to a point, whereas not having money will definitely make us unhappy. Once again, the route to sadness seems to be more reliable than the route to joy.

Of course, some of the stuff money can buy is shallow and irrelevant. A plutocrat's enormous yacht, for instance, may be regarded as an absurd and ugly thing by some, but it does fulfil the function of announcing to the world that its owner has incalculable wealth. For the shy millionaire, this would be a drawback, but a more expansive magnate will enjoy the notoriety and perceived status afforded by the yacht, precisely because it is so excessive, like the feathers of a peacock. Like that recurring film scene in which one of the characters, who is in a celebratory mood, calls the waiter in a restaurant and orders "the most over-priced champagne you have in your list!" The point here isn't to enjoy the superior qualities of the expensive champagne, but to *know* that one is spending a lot of money on it. The actual spending is the point, so money is, in this instance, literally buying happiness.

The relative value of money reminds me of Vladimir, the man in the first chapter who couldn't afford a private jet, unlike others in his social circle. I lost track of him for some time. When we met once again in clinic, he seemed more serene than on previous occasions, more at peace with himself. He wanted to consult with me about some minor possible side-effects he was experiencing from his medication, but he was otherwise well.

"You know how I used to envy my friends and their private jets?" he starts. "Well, I found out that in both cases the planes were leased, they didn't *own* them."

I hadn't realised that there is such a substantial difference between the owning and the leasing of private planes, but the distinction seems to be very significant for Vladimir. Also, I hadn't realised that this particular *jet society* had a membership of just two.

"So, anyway, I agreed with one of my friends to lease this plane jointly, so now I can say, I suppose, that I, too, have a private jet."

Vladimir concludes, apparently pleased, and yet I notice that his smile is ever so slightly forced, and a little stiff.

"Congratulations!" I say. "You must be very pleased."

"I am."

Pause.

"But, you know, it is a very expensive business leasing a plane, even jointly with someone else, and yet whenever I have the opportunity to show off and say to someone that I have a plane, then I feel the need to explain and qualify that I don't own it outright, that I lease it with a friend... and this sort of defeats the point, don't you think?"

Vladimir reflects for few seconds and then adds:

"At least, I don't feel as if I'm a failure because my friends have done better than me. That's progress, I suppose."

I can't think of anything to say. I fear Vladimir is destined to feel perpetually dissatisfied as far as aeroplanes are concerned.

We saw at the beginning of the book that millionaires always want more money, even when they have already more than they could possibly spend in several lifetimes. When money becomes an objective in itself, rather than a means of acquiring goods and services, then no amount of money, however large, will satisfy. Unlike actual goods and services, that very often disappoint or end up boring us, money has the magic charm of the potential, only limited by the amount of money available. This charm is therefore limitless in the case of billionaires. It is concrete and tangible, unlike power or recognition, and yet it remains pleasantly abstract until its potential is realised. We have also seen that income and happiness only correlate to a certain point. And yet, despite all this, there is evidence that at the very top of the wealth distribution, very rich millionaires are happier than those with only a modest number of millions in their accounts. A study published by Harvard Business School examined the levels of happiness of several thousand millionaires and found that among the very rich, being even wealthier was associated with greater happiness, a phenomenon that wasn't observable among the only moderately well-heeled. Fat cats are a happier lot than the more parochial small-time millionaires, who probably spend some of their time lamenting their relative deprivation. The study also found that earned wealth made their owners happier than those who simply inherited it.

At the opposite extreme of the lust for money dimension is Diogenes, the 5th century BC Greek philosopher, who was one of the original Cynics and a proto-Stoic. Cynics felt very positively about nature and living a life of virtue, but it was their scornful and nihilistic attitude towards things most people value (which included pretty much anything other than virtue and nature) that earned them their reputation in modern language as being "cynical". The first significant event we are aware of in Diogenes' life is a deliberate sabotage of money: he was banished from Sinope, the city in Asia Minor where he lived, after being accused of deliberately debasing their coins.

As a result of this scandal, he lost all his earthly possessions, which he never bothered to try to recover. Instead, he became a sort of classical times extreme hippie.

There are a number of possibly apocryphal stories about Diogenes that give us a flavour of the extent to which he despised wealth, social status and even any kind of standard conventions. The most famous tale refers to his encounter with Alexander the Great when he visited Corinth and met Diogenes, who was sunbathing at the time.

Now, Alexander wasn't called "the Great" for nothing; he was the most powerful and celebrated person in human history up to that point, who had conquered much of the known world, and he was about to meet a half naked chap lounging in the street, who had gained some notoriety due to his philosophical contrariness. Alexander asked him if there was anything he could do for him. Diogenes replied, "Yes, move over a little; you are blocking the sun".

Diogenes lived in a ceramic barrel, had literally no belongings of any kind, and detested any established institutions, including the family. He had the saintly and irritating habit some holy men have of denouncing others, while occupying a high moral ground himself. He would famously walk around the market in daylight with a lamp, to help him "find an honest man". He would apparently defecate in the theatre and masturbate in public whenever he felt the urge. His death may have been caused, according to some accounts, by eating raw octopus.

Diogenes' denunciation of vanity, greed, and social posturing could be interpreted, ironically, as a type of social posturing in itself. After all, he became famous by opposing established rules and values, and the persona he adopted allowed him to behave exactly as he pleased at all times. So, if Diogenes was happy, as the accounts of his life appear to suggest, perhaps it was the paradoxical social respect he gained, and freedom from work and responsibilities, that made him happy, rather than his frugal, ascetic life.

There is a syndrome in psychiatry named after Diogenes, which is applied to those who live in absolute squalor as a result of certain chronic mental conditions. It seems likely that Diogenes himself may have had schizoid traits. Having visited many Diogenes at home, often at the request of Social Services, I can attest that there is nothing attractive to be found in squalor, but I will spare the reader the details. Suffice to say that people who are driven to live in extreme poverty by their mental illness certainly don't find any comfort in their deprivation and withdraw from others because they perceive the world as hostile and threatening. I once met a lady who was so afraid of the world that she felt the need to carry all the legal documents she had ever possessed in a shoulder bag, which she constantly carried, even inside her rubbish and excrement-filled flat. The bag was so heavy that it eventually dislocated her shoulder, and yet she continued carrying it, hanging from a sagging joint that was visibly lower than her other shoulder. This lady was tormented by fear and had not found solace in poverty and withdrawal from the world.

If money and wellbeing correlate with each other to a certain extent at an individual level, could there be an association between the two at a national level too? Could there be a relationship between the average happiness of the citizens of a nation and the mean income of that country? International surveys on happiness tend to put Scandinavian countries at the top of their happiness rankings. The inhabitants of these countries have a high income, but they also enjoy high levels of social equality. One feels intuitively that being rich and being equal are both good things, but the measurement of collective happiness is fraught with difficulties. For instance, a British person approached by a stranger with a clipboard in the street would feel that the polite thing to answer will be "yes, of course", when the stranger asks her if she is happy. After all, the stranger doesn't want to know about her troubles. Meanwhile, a Portuguese person might emphatically confess she is very sad and see this as an opportunity to express culturally sanctioned feelings of *"saudade"* (nostalgic sweet melancholia, which turns up in many of their songs). Different nations have, in any case, different expectations: *"Man does not strive for happiness, only the Englishman does"*, said Nietzsche.

The United Nations has published a "World Happiness Report", which provides an answer to the question of whether wealthier countries are happier: they are. The three countries that rank highest in the 2020 World Happiness Report, as measured by six key metrics (which admittedly includes income itself, but also factors like healthy life expectancy, social support, freedom, corruption and generosity) were Finland, Denmark and Switzerland. Zimbabwe, South Sudan and Afghanistan were at the bottom. The report also found that people in cities tend to be happier then country folk. One of the chapters is entitled "The Nordic Exceptionalism", referring to the fact that Scandinavians always do so well on this kind of thing. In contrast, the 2017 Gallup Global Emotions Report concentrated on different metrics, which moved away from income and focused on positive emotions and relationships. This report found that South American countries did much better than rich but cold Northern Europeans on positive emotional domains.

Most governments vow to promote the wellbeing of their citizens by taking measures that they claim will improve their income, health, education and safety, all necessary surrogates of happiness. Big-mouthed and grandiloquent as they all always are, they still don't dare to claim that they will make their people *happy*. Not so the government of Bhutan, in the Eastern Himalayas, where the concept of "Gross National

Happiness", or GNH, has been enshrined in the Constitution as the objective of the Bhutanese government. The domains upon which GNH is based are all very good things (ecological and cultural diversity, community vitality...), but these are conveniently woolly areas for a government accused of a variety of human rights abuses, which include allegations of gross ethnic discrimination. I have no doubt at all that the Bhutanese people want, at the end of the day, what everyone else in the world wants. They want prosperity and they want safety, and they don't want, I'm equally sure, a government that tells them that prosperity is only a relative thing (Bhutan is one of the poorest countries in the world), or a government that discriminates against them if they happen to belong to an ethnic or religious minority and that curtails their freedom of association and expression. The ID card system illustrates this point well. There are seven possible citizenship categories in the ID card, but only Category 1 is for "genuine Bhutanese citizens". In any case, it is not the business of any government to promote happiness. This is an impossible quest for an individual, let alone a group of politicians and officials behind departmental desks.

The Bhutanese are not the only ones to have made happiness a national concern. *"Life, Liberty and the pursuit of Happiness"* are the three unalienable rights included in the American Declaration of Independence, inspired in John Locke's *"careful and constant pursuit of true and solid happiness"*. Pursuing this elusive goal, chasing the dream, is, not coincidentally, a very American concept, exported to the rest of us through the vehicle of American popular culture and cinema. Having the right to pursue happiness was not the same as having the right to acquire it, of course. The American Dream eventually became the equivalent of happiness to be chased, and this turned up to be a substantially material dream, made out of things, stuff and money, the essential and very mundane components of a reverie that we all have the "unalienable right" to hanker after.

The American Declaration of Independence also inspired *The Pursuit of Happyness*, a rags to riches film based on a true story. The homeless protagonist, played by Will Smith, has to compete with other unpaid interns in order to become a rich Wall Street financier. He has no income, so he subjects his young son to a destitute life together while the competition between the interns lasts. He could have given his son a roof over his head by tossing burgers instead, but big risks and sacrifices are required in the pursuit of happiness. The message here is the opposite to that of the fairy tales: you can make it big in life if you believe in yourself, even if you are a black and homeless single parent in America. And yet, instead of celebrating the anomaly of a deprived person becoming rich, we should reflect on the fact that this story is attractive precisely because it is so exceptional. The vast majority of those who are born on the wrong side of the tracks in America never make it to the other side, as studies on social mobility (or lack thereof) in that country have consistently demonstrated. The inalienable right to pursue happiness sounds a little hollow with this statistic in mind.

Money, we all agree, can't buy happiness. It is however a necessary, albeit insufficient, requirement for wellbeing. It can't get you a soul, but as George Bernard Shaw observed, *"A soul is a very expensive thing to keep"*.

CHAPTER 8

PREACHERS SAY IT'S OUR FAULT

If one googles "happiest man in the world", the name Ricard Matthieu, a renowned French Buddhist monk, comes up unanimously in scores of websites. The Internet agrees on this, so it must be true. Monsieur Matthieu himself disputes his title, arguing that he has met other Buddhist monks who are even happier than him. It is clear, in any case, that Ricard is on the better side of the happiness distribution graph of the world population (according to him, anyway), undoubtedly quite far away from where I would be found in the graph, I'm afraid, or, for that matter, most other people.

Some of these websites and newspaper articles explain that a variety of scientific tests involving EEGs and brain three dimensional functional imaging have demonstrated that during meditation the brain's good rhythms become more prominent in the EEGs, and the happy geographical spots light up merrily in the brain scans. Some journalists go on to find a connection between these findings, Ricard's participation in the studies, and the whole idea of happiness, kindness and compassion, which I find a little difficult to follow, I have to say. Incidentally, "compassion" is, to be precise, a type of suffering, so it's certainly not related to happiness. Etymologically, it means *suffering with.*

I actually admire Matthieu and his fellow happy monks very much and I have no doubt that there is a lot we can learn from them as far as our general attitude to life is concerned, but at the same time I can't help feeling a tad sceptical about any efforts to underpin or validate a philosophy or a religion with science. However, I do find the results of one particular study on meditation and the brain in which Matthieu participated, conducted at the University of Wisconsin, very interesting. The results of this experiment highlight how immensely difficult it is to control the emotional mechanisms buried inside our minds. The study found that mindfulness meditation reduced the reactivity of the amygdala in the brain (the emotional ganglion in the centre of the brain we described in a previous chapter), although, curiously, meditation dulled the reactions to positive stimuli (photographs with a pleasant theme) more clearly and sooner than its reactions to negative signals (unpleasantly themed photographs). Only the very experienced meditators, those with over 9,000 flight hours of meditating practice, managed to tame their negative amygdala reactions effectively. This brings to mind the biological bias we commented on earlier in the book. Biologically, we are meant to remain vigilant about any bad stuff around us, any risks or threats, and our amygdala is there to shout its warnings at us, like a very excitable car parking sensor that is almost impossible to switch off.

Buddhism teaches that our suffering stems from our attachment to the impermanent, and many other moral codes, religions and philosophies, from Greek Stoicism to Christianity, state that there is a moral reason for our unhappiness. This dissatisfaction is the result, they say, of our own moral shortcomings, selfishness and materialism. They teach us that we can reach a state of virtuous psychological balance through renunciation, detachment and holding back desire. Buddhism however acknowledges the reality of suffering and explains that trying to avoid pain will also produce suffering, which seems self-defeating to the uninitiated.

In an article published in the *Los Angeles Times*, the British essayist Pico Iyer observed that Americans have many more Nobel laureates but fewer patents than the Japanese. Iyer argues that this is because Americans want to chase happiness by remaking the whole world, while the Japanese acknowledge the reality of suffering and just want to *"fashion small things perfectly in corners"*.

Undoubtedly, it is a good idea to live in the moment and to detach ourselves from fear, while Buddhism's denunciation of craving and desire as the source of much of our unhappiness is also persuasive. There is, however, certain circularity in these instructions, in that the best position from which one can manage this level of detachment is happiness itself. From this perspective, the secret of happiness is simply to be happy. Once you are already happy, detaching yourself from the temptations of the world and living in the present moment, or in any other moment, will be a piece of cake.

Jesus's kingdom was not of this world, and this still shows in Christianity's condemnation of worldly pleasures and its fetishism of suffering, sacrifice and martyrdom. The "Vale of Tears" in which we live is only bearable because of the promise of what may come afterwards, although heaven is far from certain, even for a believer. It is ironic that Jesus himself preached a care-free life *("Consider the lilies of the field...")*, but somehow his religion became a discipline, a never-ending task that adopted the image of his awful torment as its symbol. Nowadays there are much jollier versions of Christianity, of course. In fact, there are different versions of Christianity available that will satisfy, and be congruent with, any philosophical or political approach to life one may care to mention, from the apocalyptic to the mindlessly optimistic, and from the far right to the far left (with a certain predilection for the right, one must say).

There is certain amount of evidence that religious people may be happier, although not every study has reached the same conclusion. It has been suggested that religious diversity in a given society diminishes wellbeing in that group and that it is the spirituality component of the religion, and not the demands it makes on the conduct of its followers, that makes the religious experience a happy one. On the other hand, a large study carried out in Switzerland a few years ago found that practising believers are happier than the non-practising ones (who were comparatively as miserable as the non-believers), which puts more emphasis on the behavioural and social aspects of the religion. Having said this, half-hearted believers are probably less likely to bother attending church on Sundays than those with deeper beliefs.

Statistical association is not causation, so the fact that religious people may be happier doesn't mean that it is necessarily their religion that is doing the trick. Perhaps the crucial factor is the belonging to a group and the sense of security this confers, or perhaps people with a happier disposition are more likely to accept a transcendental interpretation of their existence, or perhaps, finally, those who are lucky enough not to have suffered serious traumas or losses in life, and are therefore happier than those who have, are more likely to maintain a faith in a benign deity, although it goes without saying that countless people find strength in their faith in times of adversity.

Something the different religions and moral philosophies have in common is the belief that what is really important is ensuring that we live "a good life", rather than just have a good time on Earth while we are here. We saw earlier in the book that the utilitarians Jeremy Bentham and John Stuart Mill saw human happiness primarily as a mere excess of pleasure over pain, but in classical Greece, Socrates, Plato and Aristotle believed that there was another crucial and very necessary dimension in human wellbeing: according to them, happiness isn't just about *enjoying* life (easier said than done, anyway), but also about *living well.* As to what would constitute living well exactly, there is no clear agreement, but reading the different interpretations, one gets a general gist that it is a question of living in virtue and doing things that are worthwhile doing.

Pleasure can be hard to obtain, at least in substantial quantities. Hedonic, pleasurable wellbeing isn't necessarily *easier* than *Eudaimonic* wellbeing, which is the name the ancient Greeks gave to their virtuous "good life", even though the comparison of the two inevitably evokes images of a virtuous uphill and difficult path (*Eudaimonia*) versus a comfortable stroll along the sinful path of pleasure. *Eudaimonia* isn't all about virtuosity in the moral sense of the word. Some uncontrollable factors also play a part. Aristotle thought, for instance, that being exceedingly ugly (which arguably applies to a good proportion of the human race) would be an excluding condition for achieving *Eudaimonia.*

When I was in medical school in Northern Spain, very many years ago, the sinful hedonistic path seemed not only more attractive but also a lot harder in real life than the more virtuous alternatives. More than once I found myself having to reject approaches by recruiters from an organisation called Opus Dei, an ultra-conservative branch of the Catholic Church with a very poor social image because of its links to the recently defunct Franco regime. It seemed at the time that their primary purpose was to steer young lads like me away from having premarital sex. This was a repressed society even in the mainstream, with few precious outlets available for the satisfaction of the sexual appetites of young people. I found it hilarious that these zealots seemed to think that the one task that required energy, skill and commitment was that of *renouncing* sex. Instead, sex was so hard to come by that every ounce of vigour and ingenuity young men like me had was invariably, exclusively, and passionately channelled towards increasing the likelihood of *obtaining* sex. Unsuccessfully, of course.

But if seeking pleasure is hard work, the *Eudaimonic* virtuous life is no piece of cake either. It is all very well to say, as the *Eudaimonic* Stoics[10] philosophers did for example, that we shouldn't allow ourselves to be controlled by our desires and fears, but the inescapable fact is that our emotions are there precisely because they are *meant* to control our lives. Desiring pleasure and being afraid of pain are not optional features in a human life that one will be able to contain by adhering to a set of virtuous precepts; they are integral parts of being human and serve very specific functions that facilitate our survival. Stoicism is a perfectly valid way of facing the adversities of life, as the very effective British tradition of the "stiff upper lip" demonstrates, but all these moral, philosophical and religious efforts to control unpleasant emotions go *against the grain of our own nature.*

Let us use an example to illustrate this point. If we found ourselves in the Arctic tundra in the open air, we would be well advised to attempt to light a fire in order to warm ourselves up, even though any warmth so obtained would go against the prevailing climate in the Arctic. Keeping warm in that latitude in the open air will be a constant struggle, and probably a losing one. Lighting the fire will be a good thing to do, but its momentary warmth won't imply we were wrong to feel cold, and the cold temperature will remain the dominant theme, despite the fire. Similarly, some moral philosophies and religions may help control unpleasant emotions to a certain extent, but this doesn't mean those emotions are mistakes, or the manifestation

10 They were called stoics because Zeno taught this philosophy at the north portico (or "Stoa") in the Athens market.

of any moral shortcomings. These difficult emotions are the dominant climate in our mind, like the cold in the Arctic.

Despite our inevitable feelings of guilt and inadequacy, which the Christian religion has embedded in the Original Sin, unhappiness is not our fault. It is the fault of our natural outline. It is in our blueprint.

CHAPTER 9

JOY THROUGH SUFFERING?

A fairly basic and low-tech function one has to carry out as a psychiatrist is that of trying to convey hope and a sense of cautious optimism to those who are suffering with a troublesome mind. Most patients go along with this, sometimes I feel out of politeness, as a way of acknowledging my efforts to make them feel a little better. But not all. Trevor, for instance, will not accept any words of encouragement and will vehemently dispute any possible interpretation of his personal circumstances that is not entirely negative and pessimistic.

Trevor is a thin man in his early sixties, who used to work as a hospital porter, but retired on ill health grounds not long ago. He looks always downcast and talks in a monotonous voice, and at length, about how unspeakably bad every single aspect of his life is, transmitting a sense of solid, dense, constant, opaque, autonomous, unreactive and unremitting misery. He is chronically depressed, needless to say.

"So, how are you doing?"

I ask Trevor because I have to ask, and not because I'm looking forward to the answer.

"Awful, doctor," he says, predictably.

"Can't be all that bad, surely? Your GP tells me in a letter that your blood pressure has improved with the new medication, your daughter got married, and the issue with your pension has been sorted..."

"The blood pressure tablets give me side-effects..."

"What side-effects?"

"Never mind, they give me side-effects; my daughter has married an idiot; and the pension people say the issue's been sorted because they won't listen to me, so they don't even know what I'm unhappy about, and also..."

"C'mon," I interrupt, "let's try to be a little more positive, I see that in the questionnaire you filled in the waiting room you ticked that you have been sleeping a little better lately, for instance."

"Did I? No, my sleep is *terrible!*"

Trevor responds emphatically, eager to correct a positive note that he had inadvertently let escape his pen when he completed the questionnaire.

"In fact, I meant to tell you, I don't think I have ever slept so badly. Tossing and turning the whole night long, that's all I do. I don't think I have slept *at all* in the last week, and to make it worse..."

I should explain that I don't want to minimise Trevor's pain, even if I do find him ever so slightly irritating at times. I do believe he is depressed and I feel genuine compassion for his sadness. I suspect he is secretly terrified that I will decide one day he is cured and then our team will abandon him, and this is why he needs to insist so frequently that everything in his world is resolutely and constantly bad. In a way then, his pain fulfils the function of avoiding abandonment.

Pain is inevitable, so if we have no option but to live with it, perhaps we should utilise it and sublimate it into something useful. Could pain not just be useful, but also lead to a state of contentment, as some religious traditions have suggested?

"...we rejoice in our sufferings, knowing that suffering produces endurance, and endurance produces character, and character produces hope"[11]

The quote is by St. Paul. It is a laboured syllogism that progresses from suffering to hope, itself a proxy for happiness. The modern psychological equivalent is the idea of "growth" after trauma, although adapting and coming to terms with suffering, or even growing psychologically after a trauma, is obviously not the same as reaching a state of wellbeing through suffering. It is of course legitimate to try to use a painful experience for a good purpose if we can, but this is no easy task, as we shall see later in the book, and in any case, a sublimated pain is still essentially a pain at the end of the day.

Could pain be used as a creative energy? Beethoven always comes to mind when this possibility is considered. A French writer called Romain Rolland admired Beethoven very much, not just because he regarded him as a good composer, but more specifically because Beethoven, in his opinion, was able to transmit with his music the *"joy of ordeal, of pain, of battle"*, as he put it in an essay he wrote in 1927. The best known fact in Beethoven's biography is the sudden onset of his deafness when he was still young and the suffering he had to endure as a result of this loss, a particularly ironic misfortune for a musician. A sudden calamity is always a salient fact in a biography. Curiously however, the best known piece Beethoven ever wrote was on a subject opposite to loss and sadness: the choral music to Friedrich Schiller's *Ode to Joy*, in the final movement of his Ninth Symphony. We can say that Beethoven managed to "grow" psychologically after his deafness, but whether his creative genius was the direct result of his life struggles is a

11 Romans 5:3-4

different matter altogether. One can legitimately speculate that had he been born in a happy family, and had he not lost his hearing, and had he found a life companion to alleviate his loneliness, he might have been even better disposed to write beautiful music. He would certainly have been a happier man.

Other thinkers have recognised that suffering is an integral component in every human life. Some even considered it to be not just unavoidable, but indeed necessary for a complete and meaningful human experience. Nietzsche, specifically, seemed to be particularly appreciative of all the possible varieties of human anguish and torment, to which he attributed life-enhancing qualities. His manly philosophy demanded a constant struggle and despised serenity and peaceful accommodations. He wished those who were of any concern to him:

> *"suffering, desolation, sickness, ill-treatment, indignities [...] that can prove today whether one is worth anything or not — that one endures".*

We need to be clear however that his philosophy recommended generous doses of pain and affliction in order to have what he considered a fulfilled life, *not* a happy one. Fulfilment and happiness are evidently two very different things. A soldier suffering in the trench may feel he is fighting a very worthwhile and noble battle, but he is still suffering.

If Friedrich Nietzsche did genuinely desire to have the opportunity to grow as a man by facing adversity, then destiny generously granted his wishes. He developed a serious mental illness at the age of 44, the onset of which was a public disturbance in the streets of Turin, when he embraced the neck of a horse that was being flogged by its owner, in an attempt to defend it, and then collapsed. From here on, his life was a sad sequence of psychosis and strokes, until he finally reached the end of his days in the year 1900, at the age of only 55. It has been suggested that he may have had syphilis of the brain, but also that he perhaps had a bipolar disorder followed by a degeneration of the arteries of the brain, as two independent illnesses, which made him first paranoid and then confused as well. We can't be sure, of course. However, the possible manic episodes of this hypothetical bipolar illness might help explain the development of the concept of the self-sufficient "Superman"[12], a highlight of his philosophical career. It is clear, in any case, that Nietzsche didn't see happiness as the ultimate goal in human existence.

Nietzsche was, of course, an outsider who criticised the culture within, even though he became enormously influential after his death[13]. He is seen, even today, as a difficult and provocative philosopher, with a name impossible to pronounce, tainted by mental illness and associations with proto-fascists, and at odds with the simplistic ethics that most of us hold in our minds.

A common and vaguely formulated ethical belief the average person has is that well-being is a just recompense for those who behave well and pursue morally good objectives in life. However, bad things happen to good people and the experience of victimhood illustrates this point well. It is often assumed that aggressors, bullies specifically, are always troubled and unhappy individuals and that their unhappiness is the reason why they behave the way they do. But while there is no doubt that the bullied always suffer, the evidence showing that the bully also suffers is much patchier. As in the case of those narcissists who seem to be perfectly happy admiring themselves at the expense

---

12 Übermensch in German, which contrary to some reports, had nothing to do with later Nazi ideology. Nietzsche was an anti-nationalist and despised anti-Semitists.

13 "Some men are born posthumously", he wrote.

of others, many bullies are also quite content tormenting others and feeling powerful in the process.

Could a severe misfortune improve the odds of a better hand the next time around? A roulette player may think that after five consecutive reds, the next spin must surely fall on black, following what has been named the "Monte Carlo Fallacy". Of course, the odds for black will remain precisely 50% in every single spin, however many consecutive times the ball has landed either on red or on black. On August 18, 1913, the ball fell on black 26 successive times at the Monte Carlo Casino (hence the name of the fallacy). The odds of this happening were ridiculously low, so perhaps not surprisingly, gamblers in the casino bet heavily against the ball landing on black during this streak, some losing fortunes in the process. Similarly, we may think that an unusually bad patch in life is likely to be followed by an unusually good one.

After severe flash floods devastated Bilbao, my hometown, in the summer of 1983, killing scores of people as the Nervión river burst its banks during a colossal storm and waters rose very suddenly through the old quarter buildings, people from all over Spain rushed to buy national lottery tickets issued in Bilbao in the belief that God, or destiny, would surely want to compensate the city for the tragedy it had just suffered. This divine compensation never materialised. The lottery *"Gordo"* prize went to the inhabitants of some other undeserving city. Hardship didn't pay.

My friend's elderly aunt was very pious. Hers was a very stern and disciplined sort of piety, one that accepted and even embraced suffering. She attributed moral and spiritual properties to all kinds of pain and encouraged anyone who suffered to remember the saints and how some of them had bravely endured torment, and how even Jesus himself had been crucified to atone for our sins. She often mentioned St Thomas whenever this issue came up. I think this was St Thomas Aquinas, who apparently had a lot to say about suffering. Then she developed arthritis. The poor woman was in constant and agonising pain, which the drugs she was taking were unable to control.

"Remember St Thomas, auntie. That will help you tolerate the pain", recommended my friend in a mild and sympathetic tone.

"Fuck St Thomas! What did he know about pain? He didn't have arthritis!!"

So we have established that pain is painful, even when sublimated, and that suffering in the present won't improve the future. But pain may have another, more immediate, function, as many "inspirational" quotes on bumper stickers remind us. It can be the rain that makes us appreciate the sunshine, the appraisal day at the office that validates the day at the beach, the wholegrain, unsweetened muesli that allows us to look forward to the steak. These silly bumper stickers imply that we are only able to value good things by contrasting them with the bad ones, which curiously has the effect of attributing an absolute value to the bad stuff and a mere relative value to the good. Not very inspirational.

Next time I see Trevor in clinic, he looks different. His face is not the gloomy face I am used to, which portrays a standard kind of gloominess, as if it had been painted on a cartoon character. This time his expression conveys a deeper, and yet somehow more serene, sadness. It is also a more personal sadness, one that belongs to him specifically and not to the human species in general. There is a short silence before he says:

"Iris died."

Iris was his long-suffering wife, a very patient and sweet-mannered lady, who was in every possible respect the opposite of Trevor, particularly so in her incessant, half-full glass, optimistic take on life. I had only met her a couple of times, but I remember her fondly.

"I am very sorry to hear that," I say quite sincerely. "How are you bearing up?"

"You know doctor, it all happened quite suddenly, and yet I feel as if I had been expecting this for years. I miss her desperately, but oddly, I don't think I am more depressed than usual. Perhaps it's because I am still talking to her all the time, even at night."

Trevor has said all this calmly and without the sense of urgency and irritation that used to characterise his interactions with me. I see two little tears in the corner of each eye that stay there, as symbols of a sadness that stays, refusing to leave.

I think I understand the new Trevor. As he says, he had expected something like this to happen for a long time. I now see that he had a deeper insight into the true nature of life than the rest of us, which we had dismissed and misunderstood. I believe his sadness, which had been shapeless and aimless for so long, has finally found its focus in the biggest loss of his life, and with this Trevor has found a paradoxical inner peace of sorts. I know that this could be interpreted as the "denial" phase of his bereavement process, but Trevor isn't denying anything. The opposite, I feel. He is finally embracing and accepting the true meaning of his sadness.

CHAPTER 10

UNHAPPY DREAMS

Miss Brown's life has been quite awful lately. I call her Miss Brown because this is how she introduced herself to me when I visited her at home. I liked her immediately. Psychiatrists like and dislike people like everybody else, but transcend their personal emotions in order to cure their patients, including those they may not like so much, of course. No transcending effort is required with Miss Brown.

She has managed to keep her good looks and natural elegance even at her advanced age of 92. Well dressed, lovely warm voice, expressive pale blue eyes, abundant thick white hair, well judged wrinkles that describe the geometry of her face and suggest a life well lived and carefully matured, rather than impending decrepitude.

"You're going to think I've gone potty, doctor," she starts, a little embarrassed.

We are sitting at the coffee table, the cold bluish light of a winter afternoon crossing the room horizontally and then shining on the silver photo frames over the mantelpiece. The photos, some black and white, some colour, narrate a variety of travels and people, the highlights of an existence that has covered most of the 20th century, as well as a proud niece in university robes, degree in hand.

"I never had to see a psychiatrist before," Miss Brown continues, "but lately I feel as if I may be losing my marbles."

After a pause, she quietly confides:

"I've been seeing things. During the day, I sometimes feel something, a presence, can't explain it any better than that, but that's all. The problem is the nights. That's when they come out and it's terrifying."

She is looking at me intensely now, with a grave expression in her pale blue eyes.

"I know I'm old and I've had a good life, so I'm not complaining, but this I don't deserve. I see these creatures when I go to bed at night; they are like black silhouettes that sway across the room. They don't do much, but they feel really sinister. Worst of all is when I finally fall asleep because then they pull my shirt and wake me up, as if they were teasing me. But what frightens me most is the smell they bring with them, the smell of wet soil, like the smell inside a grave. A grave. That's where they come from and that's where they want to take me."

Miss Brown's experiences aren't strictly speaking dreams, but there are some clear oniric elements in them. Unpleasant dreams are a type of unhappiness for which we certainly cannot be held morally responsible. We are not accountable for whatever morally dodgy stuff happens in them, but also, and more importantly, we are not responsible for the unpleasantness that a dream may contain, as it was generated by our brains outside our conscious control. It cannot be argued therefore that a sad or distressing dream is the result of one's moral shortcomings, selfishness, and general stupidity, like with one's daytime hardships. Whatever happens in a dream, we can rest assured it isn't our fault (which, considering the weird and fairly extreme nature of some dreams, is a relief, to be honest).

Nature could have intended sleep to be a sort of time-out period, during which our brains would give us a bit of a break from our daytime torments. Instead, Nature, which abhors a vacuum, will not let the night hours go to waste when they can be usefully employed to inflict capricious ordeals on her subjects.

Sleep is "Nature's soft nurse," according to Shakespeare, but too often it is "Nature's *Nurse Ratched*"[14]. Accepting bad dreams as an inevitable fact of life, or just an unpleasant feature built into our minds, is made difficult by the fact that we don't really know *why* we dream. I was going to write that we don't know "what dreams are for", but this would be a misleading statement, as it would imply that dreaming has a function, and we simply don't know that to be the case. Instead, dreaming may be, as some have suggested, a mere random by-product of other processes that happen during sleep, without a purpose of any kind. Others have advanced different hypotheses about the possible functions dreaming may have, such as rehearsing threats and learning how to deal with them. According to this, if I have a nightmare in which I find myself engulfed by serpents while buried alive, I will then be prepared to deal with this situation when it actually happens to me in real life, although I'm not so sure screaming hysterically will achieve very much. Or perhaps dreaming helps consolidate memories or process emotional stuff that has been left unattended during the day.

Sigmund Freud was specifically concerned with the meaning of dreams and wrote a vast treatise on how to interpret them and how to uncover the *latent* (actual) meaning of the dream, to be found below the *manifest* storyline one remembers waking up. With Freud, nothing is ever obvious and meaning is always concealed under layers of mystery. Incidentally, we tend to think that anything Freud wrote was an instant sensation, but his *Interpretation of Dreams* took eight years to sell the 600 copies of the first edition, so it wasn't exactly a hit. Carl

14 She is the horrible controlling nurse in "One Flew over the Cuckoo's Nest", by Ken Kesey.

Jung, meanwhile, thought that our unconscious is trying to communicate with us when we are dreaming. It dreams in order to compensate for the rather one-sided view of things our *ego* has when we are awake, which seems to me a bit judgemental, to be honest. I take the opposite view: I happen to object to the one-sided take on things my unconscious appears to have at times, judging by the occasional awful dreams it imposes on me, and yet there doesn't seem to be a mechanism at my disposal to communicate this to my unconscious and compensate for this perceived imbalance. I would like to be able to discuss it at least.

To be able to dream, we need to sleep first, but this is a challenging task for unfortunate insomniacs, who approach bedtime with trepidation, instead of seeing the bed as a welcome relief for the weary. Again, anyone you may care to ask will probably agree that if you can't sleep, well, it's essentially your fault. As a psychiatrist, I actually find myself dishing out "sleep hygiene" advice very often, and even though I do think such advice is just and necessary, the word "hygiene" evokes the application of clinical cleanliness against some sort of less than clean, messy human vice. It is also society's fault, many people say, because of all the stresses in modern life and because the pressures of social media force us to look at our smart phones all the time, disrupting our circadian rhythm. And don't even think of taking a pill to cure your insomnia. The British National Formulary warns very sternly that hypnotics (sleeping pills) should *"be reserved for short courses in the acutely distressed"*. So if your insomnia gives you only an average kind of distress, you'll have to put up with it.

As for insomnia being the result of our frantic modern lifestyle, it is worth noting that it was very prevalent in Victorian times, when, like today, they thought of it as a modern epidemic. A neurologist called Sir William Broadbent called it *"one of the torments of our age and generation"* in the year 1900[15], the same year, incidentally, in which Freud's book on dreams was first published and then generally ignored for a long time, and also the same year Nietzsche died. Victorians were just as keen as we are to blame their ills on their times. George Miller Beard, a renowned American 19th century neurologist, thought that neurasthenia (a type of depression) was the result of *"steam power, the periodical press, the telegraph, scientific advancement, and the mental activity of women"*. I have to confess that I read this quote in E. Shorter's excellent "*A History of Psychiatry*", and not in its original source, so I'm not sure whether the "mental activity of women" made women or men neurasthenic.

If you are an insomniac, it turns out that when you finally manage to go to sleep your chances of having sweet dreams are not very good, compared to those who have no difficulties sleeping, which seems quite unfair. Having said this, good sleepers are not very likely to have that much fun while they are asleep either, as we shall see.

A psychologist called Calvin Hall, born in Seattle at the turn of the last century, had a keen interest in dreams, nothing unusual for a psychoanalyst of that period. Unlike others, however, Hall wanted to know what the general population actually dreamt about, rather than just concentrating on a handful of patients and then offering a bunch of esoteric interpretations on the latent meaning of their dreams, as Freud did. He collected dreams as others collect seashells. By the time he died in 1985, Hall had gathered over 50,000 dreams. His own college students provided many of the dream reports, but he also wrote about Kafka's and even a convicted child molester's dreams. Psychologist and author Paul Robbins explains Hall's findings in his *Psychology of Dreams*: the most frequent setting

15 Sally Shuttleworth, The Conversation, 2019.

for a dream turned out to be a plain room in a house or flat, and not the wild locations in which we imagine dreams to be staged. There were often several people in the dream, typically three. Curiously, there were very few scenes involving daily activities, such as housework, or routine working of any kind. Unpleasant emotions, such as fear, anger and sadness (in this order of descending frequency) were *twice as likely* as pleasant ones. For some reason, doors featured a lot in the dreams. There was more sex in men's dreams than in women's, but other themes were much more prevalent than sex. Dreams about being attacked, for instance, were reported much more frequently than those with an erotic content.

A few people in a room, difficult emotions, aggression, slamming doors, not doing much work... an episode of *Eastenders* comes to mind.

In case the subjects in this study had culturally-biased dreams that could not be assumed to be universal, a different author examined the dreams people had in a Mexican town called Tzintzuntzan in 1973. The excess of bad dreams, compared to the pleasant ones, was replicated in this study.

If bad or heavy dreams weren't enough, it also turns out that we have more nightmares than we think. In a study conducted about 20 years ago, a group of people were asked to keep a record of their nightmares prospectively for a month and this showed that they had more nightmares than they had estimated retrospectively as a monthly average. Not surprisingly, the author also found that these nocturnal torments didn't do the participants' sense of wellbeing any good.

Nobody, to my knowledge, has been able to demonstrate that bad dreams (remember, they are twice as frequent as the pleasant ones) have any appreciable healing properties, despite their putative psychological processing functions. For all we know, they might be just another modality of the widespread unpleasantness that colours our lives, with the aggravating factor of having no meaning and no purpose. This statement may perhaps be proved wrong one day, but we know, in any case, that Nature doesn't mind us suffering, even if it is for nothing.

I arranged for Miss Brown to have a brain scan. When acute psychiatric symptoms start out of the blue in old age, it is normally due to the degeneration of the actual brain tissue, which appears in the scan as atrophied and simply smaller than it used to be. Miss Brown's memory is perfect, which suggests that rather than a global degeneration of her brain, she may have suffered a little stroke, possibly too small to show in the scan, but enough to generate her horror movie experiences by interfering with the processing of sensory information.

The scan did show a little atrophy, but nothing spectacular, as well as some hardening of the arteries, which didn't surprise me, but no specific strokes. I didn't have to wait for the results of the scan before I gave her a small dose of an antipsychotic to take at night. This would inhibit the symptoms by dampening down the Dopamine transmission in the brain, and it would also have the added advantage of facilitating sleep. I then reviewed her in clinic.

"They've gone, the shadows have gone. Well, to be precise, I sometimes *feel* they are still there, and perhaps even see one of them in the evening, but by and large they leave me alone now".

This reminds me that she needs to have her eyesight checked. Quite often a simple cataract will send the wrong information to an ageing brain, which then has trouble processing the distorted signal, particularly in poor light. It wouldn't be the main cause of her symptoms, but cataract operations are simple and often help in these situations.

"You know", she continues, "I always slept very well, all my life, never had any trouble going to sleep and I don't think I had many nightmares, but I have always been terrified of graves and I have this thing about cemeteries, you know, I sort of believe there may be demons in them. It is as if the demons waited until I got old and frail to come and haunt me".

The 18th century etching by Goya called "*The Sleep of Reason Produces Monsters*" comes to mind. In this etching, the painter himself has fallen asleep and is engulfed by owls and bats, the creatures of the night. Miss Brown's demons had patiently waited for her to age and then for her to try to sleep. At that point, when her brain was at her lowest processing power, they came out of their tombs and haunted her.

CHAPTER 11

HAPPY EVER AFTER

I always get lost driving in this newish part of the city. For reasons that totally escape me, when the area was rebuilt in the nineteen-sixties, the purposely designed irregularity of its streets and alleys was seen as cutting edge, but my (at best) average navigating skills struggle with the wandering streets that intersect at odd angles, the suddenly changing street names (even on the same street), and the randomly allocated house numbers. Nowadays, the explicit modernity of the brutalist buildings has been disfigured by decades of decay and neglect, making this new section of town look paradoxically and pathetically old, like the architectural equivalent of a one-time very modern but now obsolete electronic gadget.

It is here that I have come to see my patient, a middle-aged lady, who lives alone at the very top of a very high tower in a tiny council flat. She is herself tiny, polite and very neatly dressed in old-fashioned housewife garments. She has a pale face ("don't go out much"), framed in short, straight white hair, and small features, but her grey eyes are sparkly and very lively. Her GP has asked me to visit her because he is worried about her isolation and wonders if this could be due to a mental illness.

She invites me into a small lounge. The views through a large window at the end of it are magnificent, but the rows of shallow and carefully numbered white shelves that cover the other three walls, floor to ceiling, are the obvious main feature in the room. I count twenty shelves in each wall, covering every single available square inch in the room, even above the door frame. In the shelves there are thousands of figurines, some made of porcelain, some plastic, all representations of fairy tale characters. I see many Snow Whites and Cinderellas, lots of carefully arranged dwarfs, long haired Rapunzels, Little Red Riding Hoods, and even several Sleeping Beauties in their clear plastic coffins. The overall effect is almost disturbing, like entering somebody else's dream, a very dense and busy dream, occupied by scores of colourful little people that have escaped from a Disney film. She notices the surprise in my expression and smiles.

"I prefer to look at them with the curtains drawn".

She switches on the rows of spotlights in the ceiling, which point at the shelves, and then closes the curtains. In the subdued light, the electric lamps emphasise the colours of the figurines and make them sparkle with warm and vibrant intimacy.

"They are my life passion. This is why I don't need to go out", she says, still smiling.

She doesn't seem to think there is a need to elaborate on this. I sense that in her mind the splendour of the fairy tale figurines is self-explanatory.

Traditional tales have often been used as vehicles for the transmission of moral values and social rules. From Aesop's Fables to the Grimm brothers' tales, the poor often have a very understandable ambition to abandon their poverty and become richer, which in these tales is seen as plain greed and tends to be heavily penalised, like in the case of *The Goose That Laid the Golden Eggs*. This fable was written by Aesop, who was a slave in ancient Greece and was described by contemporaries as being horribly ugly. No *Eudaimonia* for Aesop. The poor peasant killed the goose hoping to find gold inside it (quite reasonably, one could argue, since the goose in question kept laying golden eggs). But this man was ignorant of the fact that nothing good could possibly happen to a gold-desiring peasant in a traditional tale, so in the end he was left with no gold and no goose. Aesop, being a slave, knew not to expect too much from life.

In *The Fisherman and His Wife*, one of the tales in the Grimms' collection, a very poor fisherman catches a fish, which happens to be in fact an enchanted prince. An easy mistake to make. The man releases the fish, but his nagging wife insists he should go back and ask the fish for a bigger house and then other luxury items, and finally, drunk with the power of magic and greed combined, she declares that she wishes to rule over the earth and the heavens. These poor peasants never know when to stop, particularly older women, who in fairy tales are always unspeakably evil, so the fish/prince has no option but to punish her by taking away all the goodies he had bestowed on her and her husband. He could have stopped earlier and left things as they were at that point: nice house in a good location, perhaps a fancy carriage and a pension, but no, he had to punish them for their greed. Presumably, the fish/prince went on to confuse and tempt other poor fishermen after this, or perhaps one of them caught him one day, decided he didn't want to bother with quasi-moral, magical conundrums, and simply grilled the patronising prince in his hut the same night.

Some pretty female fairy tale characters fare better in this respect, but only by being humble and marrying a prince. This is the only type of social mobility found in fables and fairy tales. Many are already princesses at the beginning of the tale, like *Snow White* and *Sleeping Beauty*, or at least very posh, which places them in the correct social milieu for meeting and enchanting a suitable prince, who happens to be as wealthy as he is charming.

The poor girl in *The Milkmaid and Her Pail* is not a princess, which is a bad start, and being poor, she dreams of riches, so it is obvious that the tale must end in tears. She is in fact quite enterprising, if a tad naive, believing that the profit she will make on the milk she is carrying to the market will allow her to buy other goods that she will in turn sell for a larger profit, and so on. The rate of business expansion she is contemplating is a little too fast perhaps. The poor girl becomes very excited about the prospect of becoming wealthy quickly and in her exhilaration she loses her poise and topples the pail of milk she was precariously balancing on her head. Like in the case of the golden eggs, she is left with no dream and no milk. The different authors that have narrated this story over the centuries explain that the moral of the tale is that you shouldn't count your chicks before they are hatched, or that you shouldn't waste your time daydreaming about improbable improvements to your miserable life.

Underprivileged females in modern fairy tales, like Jennifer Lopez's character in *Maid in Manhattan*, or that of Julia Roberts' in *Pretty Woman,* also end up marrying lovely wealthy men, although in the case of *Pretty Woman*, he is the sort of man who indulges in a spot of rough remunerated sex after a hard day at the office. In any case, the scripts in this type of film always make it very clear that the groom's wealth is merely a happy accident, far less significant than his other charms, and yet somehow still a necessary condition.

Generally speaking, women in fiction, whether old tales or modern flicks, climb the social ladder through marriage, but the heroine never sets out to obtain an advantageous alliance; it just happens to her. Only undesirable characters, like the ugly sisters in *Cinderella*, will explicitly chase the prince simply because he is the prince. In an older version of this tale, they actually chop off their toes to make their big coarse feet fit into the delicate slipper. Not even Jane Austen's heroines, who tend to be more than a little preoccupied with money, have wealth as their primary ambition.

Traditional stories tell us that knowing your station is a good way of avoiding conflict, and that hoping to move up to a social stratum where you don't belong will only bring misery and punishment, unless you are an eligible pretty female, that is. This could be interpreted as a subtle modality of social oppression by the dominant classes, but aristocrats didn't write fairy tales. Encouraging children to forget any hopes of future riches and to accept their lot in life carries with it a deeper message: life may be crap (and if you are a peasant in the middle ages, then it most certainly *is* crap), but it may be just about bearable if you just go with the flow. It won't last very long, anyway.

It is a depressing message because of the hopelessness it instils and because it comes disguised as wisdom. It implies that there is virtue in accepting poverty and disadvantage and that ambition equals greed. On the other hand, these stories also highlight some basic truths about life that many contemporary "uplifting" films and novels with a positive message often refuse to acknowledge. Let me reveal to you, dear reader, that despite what Hollywood keeps telling us, it isn't true that we can achieve anything as long as we believe in ourselves, or that love can conquer everything. There are lots of things that we will never achieve however much we may believe in ourselves and there are also, unfortunately, lots of things love is unable to conquer. This truth is so self-evident and manifest that any attempt to expand on it or explain it would be superfluous. Equally true however is that believing that one can reach an objective and working hard at it will improve the chances of success (Carl Jung said that laziness is the greatest passion of mankind, even greater than sex) and that love is of course a crucial emotion, which we all have the need to give and receive, even though it doesn't really have any *conquering* functions. It is annoying how humans attach warring metaphors to everything, even to love, which surely is the very opposite of war.

Ali Baba, of the *One Thousand and One Nights*, has better luck. He is a poor woodcutter, and yet he manages to keep the treasures in the magic cave for himself and his family. Mind you, he steals from a bunch of thieves, which makes the whole endeavour morally palatable, and he owns a very clever female slave, so he is not that poor.

Poverty is combined with awful parenting in *Hansel and Gretel*, another tale in the Grimms' collection. Their ineffective and neglectful father is also a woodcutter, like Ali Baba, but this is where the similarities end. When famine strikes the area, he and his wife agree to abandon Hansel and Gretel in the woods, so they can keep what little food they have for themselves. The father is a little reluctant, and later regretful, but he goes along with his wicked wife's plan. Wimpish fathers abound in old tales. The children are abandoned in the middle of the Grimm brothers' mythical woods, which on top of the obvious dangers one finds in a regular wilderness, like exposure and wolves, also has horrible witches and other sinister and atavistic powers and spirits. Undeterred by the obvious and stark lack of parental competence and care, they resort to their cunning and ingenuity in order to return home, and when they are abandoned again, they return once more. They don't contemplate for a second the possibility of living anywhere else. Cruel, or at best, uncertain parenting, is another bitter and pessimistic fairy tale message, particularly prominent in the evil step-mother subgenre. In fact, one struggles to find good parents in old stories, not just in the Grimms' collection, but also in the Bible, in which Lot offers his daughters to a group of horny Sodomites and Abraham himself is ready to sacrifice his son when the Almighty demands it, for no particular reason. Hansel and Gretel love their clearly sub-optimal father (not so much their mother) and never hope to have a better one.

The shirt of a happy man is a misleading title because in this fable the happy man didn't have a shirt, which takes us back to the belief that having possessions is an obstacle to happiness. In case the reader doesn't know the story, it concerns a king (or the king's son in some versions) who fell very ill. The local sage prescribed "the shirt of a happy man" to cure his ailment. Instead of questioning such an eccentric prescription, the king's men searched the kingdom for a happy man. Curiously, there was only one in the whole kingdom. Everybody else was unhappy. Either this was a very insightful kingdom, or their living conditions left a lot to be desired, or perhaps a few were happy until an official from the castle turned up asking questions. To be fair, fables and tales only deal in absolutes, and absolute happiness is too big a concept even for a fable writer.

Anyway, the happy man was offered a lot of money for his shirt, but there were two snags: the first was that he was already happy and therefore didn't need any money; the second, and more important one, was that the happy man didn't own a shirt.

These stories are significant because our own lives, personal dramas and ambitions are represented in them. At least, this is what Marie-Louise von Franz thought. She was a Swiss analyst of the Jungian school, who thought fairy tales carry some essential truths in them. To be more specific, von Franz believed fairy tales are expressions of the "collective unconscious", which according to Carl Jung, a Swiss like her and founder of this particular school of psychoanalysis, is the part of our unconscious that is shared by everyone else in our species. It is the soul of humanity and we are born with it. This collective unconscious is populated by "archetypes", or primordial characters, some of whom turn up in old tales.

Old stories talk about what we already know, even when we first hear them as children. In their roughly textured primary colours they comment on the basic ingredients of our existence, in the form of a simple narrative. They are as raw and brutal as life and its eternal companions, love and death. Only later in life we learn to clothe our fears and desires with more refined and complex disguises. When the Grimm brothers put their collection together, they edited the saucy bits out (*Rapunzel* gets pregnant in one of the original versions) and turned some mothers into step-mothers in order to make their wickedness less shocking. More modern tales are less vicious, but also perhaps a little less evocative of our inner demons and primitive impulses.

Tales may instruct us to be pessimistic about our prospects, like in the case of the poor peasants doomed to remain destitute despite their efforts, or they may have happy endings, like in the case of the pretty princesses about to become Mrs Charming, but even here the *happy ever after* is only stated and never described. Admittedly, describing it would be very boring. After all, fiction is essentially about adversity, because life itself is about adversity, but if you stop to think about it, the task of describing a possible state of happiness that is not merely flat, unchanging and mundane, or otherwise a simple concatenation of exciting experiences, is actually quite hard. There is a sameness about the idea of happiness that makes the concept feel distant and even a little dull. This is probably the reason why it doesn't feature much in fiction. Tolstoy, who was a very tormented character, recognised that unhappiness comprises much more variety and colour than contentment in his famous aphorism, contained in his *Anna Karenina* (which is, of course, a particularly miserable novel): *"All happy families are alike; each unhappy family is unhappy in its own way."*

The time has come to say goodbye to the tiny lady at the top of the council tower and her fairy tale figurines. I certainly don't think she is mentally ill as such, although her social isolation and personality might possibly merit a diagnosis.

"It's funny", I say, after she has explained to me the method she uses to curate and organise the figurines and shown me her scrupulous cross-referential records, arranged alphabetically and thematically, "It's funny, you living here, at the top of a tower, as if you were in a fairy tale yourself".

She seems amused by the thought.

"You don't have a family, I take it?"

"No", she replies, "I've never been what you would call very social, you know. But I'm happy as I am. I have all I need here at home." After a pause, she adds: "People out there can be nasty, you know. I used to work as a typist for the Civil Service and the other girls made fun of me because of my hobby. And also because, I was, you know, different in a way, I suppose".

"You think you are different? In what way?"

"I'll tell you how I'm different", she answers instantly, with the eagerness of someone who knows an important truth about herself that needs to be said. "I'm different because I'm happy!"

I can't help feeling sceptical about her happiness, but then I reflect that perhaps I should accept it at face value. She is, after all, a princess of sorts, living in a tower, in the company of other princes and princesses, witches, midgets and dragons. Like them, she is peculiar, but through her commitment to the fairy tale, she has earned, more than anybody else, the right to be happy ever after.

CHAPTER 12

PARADISE MISLAID

In Milton's poem, paradise is lost. However, the idea of paradise as a possible destination is still with us and some even believe we'll be able to return to it after life, which suggests we may have mislaid paradise temporarily, but not irrevocably lost it.

It is curious that the Christian paradise is hardly mentioned at all in the Bible (three times in the whole of the New Testament) and there is no clear official description of it anywhere to be found. It is also curious that the descriptions that we do have of the afterlife heaven and hell – either in other religions, or in Dante Alighieri's 13th century *Divine Comedy* – are often multi-layered, with each tier devoted to a given theme, like a sort of heavenly department store.

Beatrice di Folco Portinari is believed to have been the inspiration for the character of Beatrice in Dante's journey to the heavens. She is the one who guides him through his tour of paradise, showing him all the wonders that each stage contains. In real life, Dante had a major crush on Beatrice Portinari, who lived close to him in Florence. They were both more or less the same age. She was very pretty and rich and embodied in Dante's mind everything that was blissful, beautiful and heavenly. Despite the very elaborate description of paradise in Dante's story, one has the impression that his admiration for Beatrice was such that he probably felt heaven was nothing more and nothing less than Beatrice herself. He claimed in his writings that they only met a few times, but this is difficult to believe, given that Florence in the middle ages wasn't a big place and that he allegedly used to hang out in places where he could catch a glance of her, like an infatuated teenager. But then, he *was* an infatuated teenager. He first met her at the age of nine and wrote: *"from that time forward, Love quite governed my soul"*. She was twenty five when she died.

Dante's longing for Beatrice is included here because she was, I believe, his heaven on earth, more so than the complicated concentric spheres he visited in his imagined paradise, occupied by saints, angels and other hallowed characters. A paradise on earth is the happiness we seek in vain, which is the subject of this book.

The etymology of the word "paradise" is interesting precisely because it is so much of this world. It meant "walled garden" in Old Persian, a concept that evokes the very essence of serenity, an enclosed and private portion of the natural world that is tended, curated and protected from external intrusion. This is a garden that is always beautiful, that changes and evolves according to natural cycles, sheltered and confined, tranquil and yet alive, immune and independent.

The Garden of Eden was also in this world, even though it is a mythological entity. Eden was a place where innocence and abundance were the main themes, both necessary ingredients in the magical recipe for happiness. Then innocence was lost, as we shall see in the next chapter, and Adam and Eve were instructed to work if they still fancied the abundance, or even valued their bare subsistence.

The left panel in Hieronymus Bosch's *Garden of Earthly Delights* triptych, kept at the Museo del Prado in Madrid, shows a very lush Garden of Eden, in which God himself is presenting a slightly puzzled Adam with a shy looking Eve, even though she shouldn't be aware of her nakedness, as she hasn't sinned yet.

The panel contains many fanciful animals and it is interesting to note that several of them are predators with prey in their mouths. This is certainly not a Disney romantic scene, in which all the pretty forest animals love each other. Bosch's paradise may look surreal, but it is also carnal and natural, and this even includes death itself.

Et in Arcadia Ego ("even in Arcadia, I am") is the title of another painting, this one by Nicolas Poussin, a French 17th century artist. It is held at the Louvre and it refers precisely to the fact that death is inescapable, even in Arcadia, which is another version of paradise on earth. It depicts a group of idyllic but perplexed shepherds gathered around a tombstone, apparently wondering what is such a morbid object doing in their lovely Arcadia.

A differently sexed version of himself perplexes Adam in one painting, and death perplexes the merry shepherds in the other. No paradise can last very long after it has been burdened with sex and death, as Bosch's central and right panels in his triptych explain. The central one is very sensual, all flesh and large fruit, and the one on the right is nightmarish and bizarre, presumably depicting the hellish consequences of carnal dissipation and excess. This suggests that once the first humans lost their innocence, they were only able to recreate a clumsy and coarse version of paradise based only on the delights of the flesh. This, as we well know by now, must necessarily end in chastisement, according to the rules of the "pleasure economy", as discussed earlier in the book.

I met Charlie a very long time ago, when I was a junior psychiatrist in an inner-city ward. He was a young man in his early twenties, who had been brought to the hospital on something called a Section 136 of the Mental Health Act. If a person is found in the streets behaving in a way that suggests they are mentally unwell, this section of the Act allows the Police to take them to hospital for assessment. Charlie was reported by a member of the public, who saw him standing in the central reservation of a double carriageway at night, in torrential rain.

Looking back, it pains me to remember how young, and yet how unwell, Charlie was, but at the time I wasn't much older than him, so his youth didn't shock me so much.

Psychiatric wards in the late eighties looked awful. They were grotty and generally very unpleasant places. Luckily, they have improved immensely since then. Before I went to see him in the dark and neglected communal male room, where he was occupying the bed furthest from the window, the nurse in charge had informed me that he had been virtually mute since he was brought to the ward late the previous night. He hadn't eaten, drunk, or slept at all. He remained still, sitting on the bed in a slightly awkward posture and staring blankly into space. If asked a question, he would simply reply "I have to go".

Charlie was suffering a first episode of catatonic schizophrenia, which with appropriate medication and nursing care, soon started to improve. Luckily, he started drinking fluids more or less straightaway; otherwise he would have needed ECT (electro-convulsive therapy), which is brilliantly effective at improving a catatonic episode, but also invasive.

A few days after admission, Charlie had started to talk. Not much, but this improvement was encouraging nevertheless. He still repeated he "had to go", but to the obvious follow-up question of "where to?" he finally answered: "Shangri-La".

James Hilton wrote the novel *Lost Horizon* in 1933. It is set in a Tibetan monastery in the lost and fictional valley of Shangri-La. In the novel, this monastery was a completely isolated community and yet somehow managed to possess and contain all human wisdom within its confines. As in all utopias, the inhabitants of Shangri-La were very peaceful and opposed materialism. They also lived extremely long lives. The High Lama, for instance, dies in the story at the age of 250, which isn't bad.

Actually, we are not able to state that Shangri-La is a fictional location anymore because the previously named Zhongdian County in Chinese Tibet is now officially known as Shangri-La. The name was changed in order to attract revenue from tourists looking for paradise. It is debatable whether a city that has been under what many regard as a foreign occupation since 1949 should have a claim to paradise status, however pretty the city may look in photos. Many other cities and valleys in the western Himalayas claim to be the original Shangri-La, forgetting perhaps that there was no Shangri-La when the novel was written. We shouldn't be too surprised; after all, there is also a Juliet's balcony in Verona, several statues to Quixote and Sancho in Spain, and one to Sherlock Holmes in front of Baker Street underground station in London.

Hilton, who also wrote *Goodbye Mr Chips*, appears to have been inspired to write his story on Shangri-La – at least to some extent – by the accounts of the Jesuits who travelled to Tibet through arduous Himalayas crossings in the 17th century, allured by tales of a wonderful kingdom beyond the mountains and by the mysterious maps leading to it. They were excited at the prospect of making this kingdom Christian. Evidently, these Jesuits had their own "true" paradise, but they wanted the inhabitants of any other paradise to be persuaded to believe in theirs.

Lost Horizon was an enormous success, selling many millions of copies. Some say in fact that it was the first ever paperback mass-market bestseller. Frank Capra directed a film based on it in 1937, which was also successful.

There is also a real Arcadia in the map, but unlike Shangri-La, Arcadia has always been there, in the middle of the Peloponnese peninsula. Arcadia is, even today, a very charming and idyllic-looking mountainous district that brings to mind the very image of bucolic beauty and simplicity, like Beethoven's 6th Symphony, even though it contains a city incongruously named Megalopoli, as well as a huge power station. In the Arcadia of classical times, there was harmony and there was abundance. Life flowed easy in the Arcadian valleys. Virgil, the Roman poet, set the poems in his *Eclogues* in Arcadia. Pan, the Greek mythological figure with horns and goat's legs, the satyr associated with nature, spring, nymphs and sex, lived there. This is a jolly, spontaneous, hedonistic and natural sort of paradise, not one derived from any kind of discipline and reflection. No wonder the half-goat Pan ended up personifying the Devil himself in Christianity.

Shangri-La is essentially more a Utopia than a paradise, where happiness has been arrived at through the path of wisdom. In contrast, Eden and Arcadia are simple, lush, easy and innocent. Their inhabitants didn't achieve and then carefully maintained their contentment; they happened to be happy and didn't even know that unhappiness might exist at all.

An intense sense of nostalgia permeates the concept of paradise. We feel we emerged from it in the distant past and that doing so was a simple but unfortunate mistake. We complicated our lives too much, became too ambitious, invented travel, invented credit, invented political structures, and became unhappy in the process.

Our society doesn't seem to like the present very much. We are very critical of everything modern, from technology to globalisation. Right wing voters don't like the liberality of modern times, while those on the left don't like the loss of communal values that comes with the modern pursuit of profit and expanding markets. However, nostalgia isn't a new thing. It has always been with us and, in fact, it was particularly prominent as a social sentiment in the times we now feel nostalgic about, ironically. It seems paradoxical that people in the 19th century, or even in the preindustrial societies of the Renaissance, which we see as distant and romantic and therefore detached from the mundane ugliness of our present reality, should themselves have felt so nostalgic about their own concept of a long-gone golden era. It was in the Renaissance that the myth of Arcadia became particularly popular, but long before this the writers of classical Greece themselves had felt nostalgic about a lost "Golden Age", while Victorians saw the middle ages as the romantic ideal they most wanted to emulate.

Paradise cannot be found in the map, even though Arcadia and Shangri-La can. There are also many places called Eden, of course. Many of them were developed in suburbia during the building boom of the nineteen-thirties. They offered a gardened leafy paradise away from the smoky horrors of the inner city. Ideal living has now moved back to the urban environment, so this may be Eden's new setting, in the form of a swish city-centre apartment with a mezzanine and a small balcony with views to the river.

There are also a variety of locations in the Middle-East that claim to be the original Eden, but being too flat, harsh-looking and torn by political instability, they are all unconvincing candidates for the title. In any case, paradise is, by definition, always somewhere else.

Madeira, the quiet and beautiful Portuguese island in the Atlantic with the wonderful climate and gorgeous volcanic scenery, is as good an image of paradise as any other. In the streets of Funchal, the capital of the island, I once saw in the window of a travel agent a large picture of a golden sand beach and palm trees in a colourful sunset light, with the legend underneath, written in Portuguese: *"Escape to paradise"*. Madeira has many attractions, but being volcanic it doesn't have the type of natural beach depicted in the travel agent poster. I found the ad perplexing. I thought *I* was escaping to paradise when I came to Madeira, but it turned out the inhabitants of Madeira didn't think they were in paradise at all and felt the need to escape to their own idea of paradise. I am sure that people living by the tropical beach depicted in the travel agent's window also wanted to escape to their own idea of paradise, perhaps to the city in Europe from where I had started.

Charlie continued to improve steadily, but very slowly. He started to communicate in short and disjointed sentences and, in the process, I was able to form in my mind a rough idea of what was going on inside his. One night, while I was on-call, the telephone rang in my damp and cockroach infested room. If psychiatric wards were horrible in those days, on-call rooms weren't much better. Charlie seemed very upset, the charge nurse told me, and might need some extra medication to calm him down and help him sleep. When I arrived in the ward, after crossing the desolate hospital grounds in semi-darkness, I saw Charlie, crying quietly, in the interview room where the nurse had placed him so he would not disturb the others in the dormitory.

"I wanted to go, they told me to go, I wanted to go!"

Charlie said insistently, still crying.

"I know", I said, "you told me, you had to go to Shangri-La; did you hear voices asking you to go there?"

"Yes. And now they've gone and I don't know where I should go to, or how. I'm so confused!"

"Don't worry, Charlie, you don't need to go anywhere just now. First, you need to sleep, then you need to carry on getting better, and then we'll help you find your way back home".

Charlie did eventually go back to sleep with the help of a pill and he also continued to get better steadily. In fact, he reached a full recovery. The medium term prognosis in these situations however isn't great. Many will suffer a second episode within five years and, in the meantime, Charlie's chances of functioning well in terms of work and relationships weren't that good, unfortunately. But his parents and I kept our fingers crossed.

A superficial analysis of Charlie's emotional upset the night I went to see him in the ward would suggest that before coming to hospital he had found himself in a strange psychotic bliss, expecting to be guided by his auditory hallucinations on a pilgrimage to Shangri-La, and that this happy expectation had then been frustrated by the treatment, which brought Charlie back to a painful reality. To an extent this may have been true, although there is no such thing as a sustained psychotic bliss. Emotions in psychosis tend to be either blunted, or otherwise intensely unpleasant, or at best, mixed and changeable. And Charlie did need to be brought back to reality, of course.

For a little while however, Charlie had a paradise to go to, but then, like the rest of us, he lost it, or at least mislaid it.

CHAPTER 13

LOSS OF INNOCENCE

A member of staff at the supermarket comes to validate the weekly wine purchase I have just scanned, by tapping on the *"visibly over 21"* button on the screen. The supermarket lady wouldn't hesitate a moment before tapping the button even if it demanded me to be visibly much older. There is no denying it, I'm getting on.

I have been around for a while and this has made me wiser (if perhaps not yet wise in absolute terms) and at times weary of the ways of the world. If there is one characteristic of youth I miss, it is the now long-gone innocent belief in a benign world.

In the Garden of Eden we described in the previous chapter, Adam and Eve ate the fruit (not necessarily an apple, incidentally) from the "Tree of the knowledge of good and evil" and in doing so they lost their innocence.

Innocence is capital, not income. We are born with a large quantity of it and then we steadily lose it, never to replace it again. Traumatic events that we experience in life, sometimes at an early age, impact on our ability to see the world as benign. This gradual loss of "innocence capital" promotes weariness and erodes our potential for happiness.

A young person isn't happier than an old one, but unless he has been subjected to abuse or neglect, he retains an ability that the older guy has lost: he is still able to believe that the satisfaction of his simple range of ambitions is all he will need to be happy. If my young self is anything to go by, my personal ambitions at that stage were either romantic or to do with passing exams, while continuing to be able to engage in a modest variety of assorted hedonistic activities, of course.

Young people are also quite optimistic. In fact, they are often afflicted by what psychologists call "Unrealistic Optimism", which is the opposite of the "negativity" cognitive bias we described earlier in the book. When we are young, we seem to be curiously bad at imagining horrible things ever happening to us, but the adversities we experience as we get older gradually correct this illusion. Research has shown that "positive illusions" are strongest in young people who have enjoyed a happy childhood, which isn't surprising. The negativity and the optimism biases seem to be contradictory, but they work in different domains: the negativity bias helps us remain on our toes and identify any possible threats lurking in our everyday life, whereas the "unrealistic optimism" bias helps the young get on with life and take some risks, as young people must, without being paralysed and overwhelmed by the awareness of all the awful things that could happen to them. We'll see in the next chapter that this phenomenon doesn't necessarily disappear in old age and sometimes the onset of frailty surprises an old person who hitherto had felt that old age infirmity only affected others, and surely not them.

So how is this optimism manifested? Psychologists who have studied the phenomenon explain that humans frequently have an "illusion of control" over the factors affecting events in their lives, when in fact they don't really control them, or at least they do only partially, and so they overestimate their chances of success. Our destiny is, as the saying goes, in the lap of the gods, and yet we delude ourselves that we are in charge of events. However, the older we get and the more unexpected snakes we find in the grass as life progresses, the more we realise our illusion of control is, well, only an illusion. For instance, a study found that young people who lived through the 1989 California earthquake had their optimism about ever being victim of a natural disaster tempered by that experience. They had been asked before the event if they thought this kind of thing could ever happen to them and they rejected the idea as preposterous, even though they lived in California, which is an earthquake-prone area. Their optimism in other areas remained resilient even after the earthquake, waiting to be eroded by future events.

Similarly, many studies have found that we tend to believe that we are less likely than others to develop a serious health problem. Life can be trusted to correct this misconception at some point.

In a famous study carried out in the 1970s, two American investigators looked into the possible relationship between unrealistic optimism and depression. They recruited a group of students and divided them into depressed and non-depressed sub-groups after they completed some questionnaires designed to assess their mood. Then the students were asked to press, or not press, a button that might, or might not, make a green light come on. The likelihood of the light responding, or not, to the button was predetermined. This procedure was repeated forty times. At the end, the students had to assess to what extent they thought they had been able to control the green light. The researchers found that non-depressed students over-estimated their ability to control the light, but curiously, the depressed ones were remarkably accurate. "Sadder but wiser", was part of the paper's title. This phenomenon has been termed "depressive realism".

It is probably significant that many of the studies that have found high levels of unfounded optimism (this would exclude the depressed realists above) used college students as their subjects. College students are very handy, available and very willing to participate in psychological studies, but they also very young and naive. Bless them.

In time, these college students grow older, "sadder and wiser", as they live through some of the things they thought would never happen to them, while gradually realising that they can only exert partial control over their destinies. The process is evidently painful.

We hear sometimes a person with a religious faith say that after enduring one of the ordeals that life sometimes throws at us his "faith was shaken" by the event. On the surface, this is quite puzzling; was he not aware that others before him had been victims of cancer, or abuse, or even had a loved one murdered? Had he never heard of the Holocaust? Why hadn't *that* knowledge shaken his faith?

There are in fact two different issues at play here. First is the fact that a deity that is nasty to others is more forgivable than one that is nasty to me personally. The other is more relevant to the subject of this book: we see horrible events that we haven't experienced or witnessed ourselves as freak anomalies that couldn't possibly be part of our very normal lives. They only happen to some unspecified "others", with whom we cannot sympathise to an extent that would allow us to appreciate the actual enormity of their tribulation. It would be emotionally intolerable having to sympathise fully and willy-nilly with every stranger we hear has suffered a misfortune. As a result, these misfortunes remain alien to us, and the faith in the god that allowed them to happen remains untested.

I am on my way to a home visit in a part of the city that is so furiously cosmopolitan that no particular nationality is more prevalent than any other, including the indigenous one. This lack of homogeneity continues in the streets, where every building is different and every shop front has dissonant and shouty graphics in vivid colours advertising the cuisine of Laos, Nigerian barbers, or Paraguayan family lawyers.

Maja, the lady I've come to see, is very old. She grew up in Warsaw a very long time ago. Her GP tells me in the referral letter that she has fallen prey to a gang of local criminals who gained her trust and then took all her savings. The GP wonders if she may be losing her memory and perhaps this has made her more vulnerable to abuse by strangers.

Maja is small and mild. Her deep brown eyes look tired but strangely serene. She lives alone in a very small flat, in which she managed to cram in at some point a number of big, heavy and dark brown, pieces of furniture.

Maja welcomes me warmly, even though I'm not certain yet that she has understood fully who I am or why I am there.

I have the habit of looking at the photos in the living rooms I visit. They give me an immediate context to my patient's presentation, particularly if they are confused. I see on Maja's mantelpiece a photograph in a silver frame of a young smiling girl with a man, she in a summery dress and white socks, he in a light coloured linen suit and spectacles.

"I am the girl and the man is my father."

Maja takes the photo, holding it lovingly with both her hands. After a short pause, she looks at me and explains in a soft voice and even softer accent that she lost her whole family, parents and two sisters, in the Holocaust. Only she survived. The picture on the mantelpiece had been taken shortly before her life was cruelly misshapen by the biggest crime in human history. She was eighteen when she was taken to Auschwitz.

Maja came to this country as a refugee after the liberation of the camps at the end of the war, worked as a seamstress all her life and never married.

"He was such a handsome man, my father", says Maja, still looking at the photo in her hands, "life was so simple then, and we were so innocent, even my father and mother; we had no idea what was coming".

As she places the photo back on the mantelpiece, I see the long number tattooed on her lower left arm.

I ask her about the crooks who took her money. She seems unconcerned.

"I often think I did all my suffering in the camp and there is no suffering left for me. I also have little time left at my age, and money doesn't mean anything to me now, anyway."

To my surprise, when I test her memory, it seems to be quite good. A confused person's memory often fluctuates during the day, but my feeling is that hers is good enough. It was probably her judgement that wasn't good enough when she decided to trust the criminals with her money.

"You'd think that I'd be able to spot a bad man by now, considering what I went through in my youth, but you've got to trust people, don't you think?"

I found Maja's resignation remarkable. Abuse and aggression on this scale often scar the victim irreparably by impairing their ability to believe in a benign world and the goodness of people. This is why the rate of suicide among Holocaust survivors was much higher than in the general population. Primo Levi, the celebrated Italian writer, was one of many Auschwitz survivors who met such a tragic end many years after his imprisonment. Jean Améry, the Austrian essayist, was also incarcerated and tortured in Auschwitz and took his own life years later. So did Bruno Bettelheim, the Austrian psychologist, after enduring the hardships of Dachau.

I realise that, luckily, most of us never suffered – and hopefully will never have to suffer – anything comparable to the anguish and tortures experienced by these unfortunate survivors, but their suicides are included here as an illustration of what happens to the mind when it is exposed to the darkest side of life and human nature. A person who has "known" these horrors has his perception of the world, and those in it, transformed. This person has suffered a total loss of innocence. The Holocaust was an extreme and unusual event, but it *did* happen, and so it belongs to the human race and must be understood within the parameters of our human blueprint. Any attempts to represent the human species as essentially benign must explain how the Holocaust could have occurred in a world without a malign component in its core, regardless of how exceptional an event it was. One has to conclude logically that this world is not fundamentally benevolent. Our gradual realisation of this fact, which takes place as a result of the different traumas that we suffer in life, has an irreversible impact on our ability to feel happy, even if the traumas are much smaller than what Maja suffered back in the nineteen-forties.

Viktor Frankl was an Austrian psychiatrist who also ended up in the camps, but he apparently managed to find meaning and a reason to live even in these most horrid of places. It has been reported that he had far-right nationalist sympathies before the war (ironically), as well as lifelong deep religious convictions. He wrote a book called *Man's Search for Meaning* based on his concentration camp experiences that became a huge best-seller. Incidentally, this book contains a reflection on how chasing happiness is futile: *"Happiness cannot be pursued; it must ensue"*, he says. He argues that happiness will be an unintended side-effect of one's dedication to greater causes. Greater and higher things are a recurring theme with Frankl, who didn't like Freud's obsession with the low and the deep. Frankl's belief that one could find "meaning" even in Auschwitz resonated with the positive thinking movement that has now become so prevalent in popular psychology.

Frankl's idea of meaningful suffering has been severely criticised by Timothy Pytell, a California State University professor, who claims that Frankl distorted the reality of Auschwitz (where he says Frankl only spent three days, although he was also in other camps) in order to substantiate and promote his psychological theories, and that Frankl was involved in some very dodgy experimental brain surgery on Jewish patients who attempted suicide to avoid deportation to concentration camps. These experiments were sanctioned by the Nazi regime and didn't exactly meet the highest of moral standards.

"It is naïve, absurd, and historically false to believe that an infernal system such as National Socialism sanctifies its victims", said Primo Levi.

One wonders if Frankl's book may have helped sanitise the Holocaust to a certain extent and extricate the evil that carried it out as something external to us that we don't need to explain. Levi describes in one of his books that the few who happened to survive Auschwitz weren't necessarily the best among them and did not represent the millions who died. For those in the queues walking towards the gas chambers, Frankl's search for "meaning" might have sounded very hollow.

It is beyond the scope of this book to consider whether life has a meaning, or whether we should search for it even in difficult circumstances, other than to state that there is certainly no meaning to be found in our natural, biological self, or in the natural world around us.

As a requirement for a fulfilling life, purpose is arguably a more accessible and useful concept than meaning. *"Give a man health and a course to steer, and he'll never stop to trouble about whether he's happy or not"*, said George Bernard Shaw.

Obviously, one doesn't need to be exposed to an event of historical importance to develop a Post Traumatic Stress Disorder. An accident, an aggression, or a glimpse of death can trigger this clinical disorder. Interestingly, while these events are by definition very distressing, they also tend to be relatively mundane and ordinary. We all know that one day we could have a nasty accident, for instance, but *actually* having the accident transforms this knowledge into a deeper and more immediate awareness of the fragility of life that may be very difficult to live with. It is as if we needed to put some emotional distance between us and the awful things we know are lurking out there. We need a certain degree of denial. We need a certain measure of "unrealistic optimism".

Before I leave Maja, I accept her offer of a cup of tea. This is testament of my trust in her cognitive abilities, as it is otherwise anathema for a psychiatrist to drink any beverages offered to him by a confused person in a home visit. One could only imagine the bacterial loading that such a cup of tea would carry. It is one of the mysteries of nature that confused patients seem to be strangely immune to the perils of drinks prepared with faecal matter impregnated fingers, but alas, their psychiatrists aren't. Anyway, Maja is not confused, so I am very happy to drink her tea. I also need to establish whether she may be depressed, not because I have any specific inkling that she might be, but because she is isolated and because she was subjected to such an unspeakable trauma in her youth, which is a predisposing factor for depression later in life. So I start by asking her if she thinks about the past much.

"I do, all the time!"says Maja emphatically, while pouring the tea from a very elaborate looking teapot, her brown eyes suddenly sparkling with life.

"You know, doctor, my life here has been good, but in a way my *real* life ended the day my family and I were separated and taken to the camps, or perhaps even earlier, in the ghetto. Don't get me wrong, I've had happy days in this country, but my world – our world – finished in the ghetto. My family and I lost everything at that point. We lost our way of life, our dignity. And then of course, I lost them, I lost my family. But when I say my real life finished at the ghetto, what I mean is that the life that came after this was different, it wasn't the same. How should I put it..."

Maja hesitates for a second.

"...the life that happened after I came across the evil of this world had *less value*, less substance to it, so I don't worry too much about what may happen to me now. You know what I mean?"

I think I do.

CHAPTER 14

PATCHY BIOGRAPHIES

Listening to Sinatra singing *"My Way"*, or to Édith Piaf and her *"Non, je ne regrette rien"*, always makes me feel a little jealous. Personally, I'm not so sure I am that proud of having always done things in life "my way", and unlike Piaf, I actually do regret an awful lot of stuff.

Regrets
I've had a few
But then again
Too few to mention

Interestingly, *"My Way"* was also originally a French song, which would make me wonder if there is something specifically Gallic about being a bit smug when looking back at one's life, except the original French lyrics were totally unrelated, so I can't conclude that. Shame.

Neither Sinatra nor Piaf would change a thing in the fictional biographies of their songs, but our own life histories are likely to be less satisfactory. Real lives are uneven and patchy, lovely bits juxtaposed with grim episodes we'd rather forget. Unlike Sinatra, I would personally love to be given a life editor with the power to erase all the mistakes I've made in my existence so far, and I suspect the reader of these lines would like to be given one too, if such an editor were available.

Another unsatisfactory aspect of the narrative of life is the fact that there is no dramatic crescendo as we age.

There is a concept in psychology called the "reminiscence bump", which refers to the fact that we recall our adolescence and early adulthood much more easily, frequently and intensely than any other stages in life. It has been argued that this is because those years contain so many powerful experiences and because it is during that period that we define ourselves as a person. There are however crucial experiences that come later in life and are as intense and transcendental as any of the earlier ones, like parenting, for instance. Even so, the reminiscence bump seems to be not only very real, but also universal, spanning across different cultures.

We normally peak relatively early and when the last stages of life finally arrive, we may feel surprised that the life we had was all that there was. It can feel as a bit of an anticlimax.

It's a busy clinic again and I am having trouble with this consultation; we don't seem to understand each other very well. Alfred, my patient, is finding it difficult to express what's going on in his mind. He is a well built, well dressed, neatly combed, confident looking eighty-five year old, but he is also distressed and low in mood.

It's not always obvious what we mean when we say something, even less so when one is feeling emotionally unwell and there is that emotion to convey, as well as the narrative that goes with it. Sometimes a psychiatric consultation appears to progress along two simultaneous monologues that don't intersect at all, the patient trying desperately to explain and the psychiatrist trying to understand, but both referring to different mental diagrams, different ways of believing and understanding, and using different language.

"I don't understand what's happening, doctor. I've always been very strong and never had any health problems, never in my life, but just lately I've started having trouble passing urine and my GP told me it was my prostate, then I had a couple of funny turns, to do with my heart apparently, and then my hip started hurting. My GP says it's arthritis and it's to do with age. But I don't understand, why is all this happening to me all of a sudden, when I've always been in good health before?"

"It must be very difficult having to contend with all these things coming to you more or less at the same time".

As I say this, I sense that Alfred isn't just looking for sympathy from me; he genuinely doesn't understand what's happening to him. Being ill is new to him.

"Also, there is wear and tear; you aren't so young anymore..."

I add this a bit timidly because blaming age isn't always the most sophisticated of medical arguments.

"I don't know, it's not like me, being ill. Other people get ill, never me".

I am surprised that Alfred, an intelligent man, can't appreciate the obvious connection between an advancing age and an increasingly fragile health. After the clinic, while having lunch, I consider the matter again and realise that I am looking at this issue like a doctor. To a doctor, this is about a particular age group and its corresponding epidemiological risks, whereas Alfred is not thinking in epidemiological terms; he is thinking of his own life history and his own identity.

According to psychology professor Donald Polkinghorne, seeing oneself as a story, and not a freestanding "thing", emphasises the dramatic dimension of life. He also believed that when we find ourselves under stressful conditions, this self-narrative may crumble, producing a sense of meaninglessness, which will be inevitably accompanied by anxiety and depression. So it is the life stresses disrupting the internal *"history of me"* that makes us feel distressed and anxious.

Our personal stories are enormously complex. We have episodes and chapters, some sad, others funny, some even heroic; we have myths, dangers, baddies and twists. A book by the Gestalt therapist Erving Polster has the title *Every person's life is worth a novel.* When I am in a city I have never visited before, or in a commuter train in a dark winter evening, I like looking at the windows in the apartment blocks and the illuminated rooms behind them, all of them different, each representing a contained universe of long and intricate life histories, millions and millions of memories, regrets, hopes, loves and fears, and as many novels as individuals populating those human beehives.

Unlike a novel, the storyline in a human life has a way forward, a yet unwritten future. Even when the present is threatening or unfulfilling, we can still hope. We have hope in the future, the next stop in our life narrative, because we think that life is a journey that leads somewhere, a better place perhaps. But while approaching life as a narrative may emphasise the dramatic dimension in our lives and give us a sense of "self", it also creates a distorted expectation that the end stages of life cannot fulfil. The flow of the narrative of life is almost always unsatisfactory. This is why film biopics tend to be a little awkward and always focus on particular episodes in the protagonist's life, rather than relating their whole life journey. Happiness, if it exists at all, would be corrupted by the complexities and tensions of a narrative. It would probably be better represented in a still photo than in a film.

We project our ambitions on the future and remember the past with nostalgia. In fact, it has been argued that happiness can only be remembered, rather than experienced, and that reflecting on whether we are happy in the present moment will inevitably break the spell. This is why George Bernard Shaw advised us against having any leisure time in which to wonder about such things.

We also reminisce about the past. Nostalgia is a powerful emotion. "Any time gone by was better", observed the Spanish poet Jorge Manrique, demonstrating that nostalgia is a universal feeling, to which not even a young man in the 15th century was immune. We remember the past fondly because being constant and permanent it is also unthreatening, unlike the present and the future. Some of our fondest memories have been mythologised and filtered so heavily, that no amount of present bliss could possibly compete with them. The balding husband snoring gently on the sofa, with the TV control still in his hand and dribbling a little bit, doesn't have a chance against the memory of that other young, smiling and tanned lover in a distant Mediterranean holiday, except he too may be balding and asleep on the sofa by now.

In fact, we are not very good at judging how much we have enjoyed, or not, a given experience in the past. This is influenced by the so-called "peak–end rule", which means that we tend to judge, say, a holiday, according to how we felt at its most intense moment, disregarding how we felt during most of the holiday. In this way, that trip to Lanzarote boils down in our memory to just one fun beach party, while the other average and slightly boring thirteen days abandon our consciousness. The peak-end rule also applies to longer segments in our lives, reducing whole relationships, for instance, to a few colourful occasions.

Research into nostalgia has found this emotion to be quite useful: reminiscing nostalgically not only helps strengthen social bonds, but also increases positive self-regard and generates positive affect. It has been claimed that nostalgia can even increase a sense of meaning in life (no small feat), by promoting feelings of social connectedness.

Nostalgia may be comforting, but the past we miss will never return, and it probably was never that wonderful anyway. The future, not the past, is our destination. It is the place where our hopes live, where all the shortcomings of the present time are resolved and where the threats and fears that torture us now will finally be placated.

Heraclitus famously remarked that one cannot step into the same river twice, as a way of illustrating the fact that we live in a constantly changing world. Heraclitus was a classical Greek philosopher, known in his time as "The Obscure" because of his tendency to speak in riddles, a very irritating habit some very deep thinkers have. He was also prone to depression, so apart from the famous river aphorism, his musings tend to be neither cheerful nor very clear. We have to agree with him however on the fact that our personal circumstances are endlessly mutating. These persistent changes will never allow us to fix everything that is wrong in our lives and reach a point in which we can declare that all is well. Our present anxieties will inevitably be replaced by our future anxieties, in a never ending trial that is impossible to win.

The future isn't the abode where happiness resides, but it does contain something that is absolutely certain and provides a definitive solution (of sorts) to all our problems: death.

None of us really, *deep down*, believe we are going to die. Not *me*, surely. Every single time I have checked so far, I was alive, which is a very powerful statistic.

Sigmund Freud believed that humans don't accept their mortality, and yet he also described his controversial "death instinct", in which "the aim of life is death".

Death is the least exclusive of all clubs, and yet our awareness of it is so poor that we need *memento mori* to remind us of its inevitability. Well, *we* don't need them; people in the past did. Modern man doesn't like thinking about death, so he doesn't need to be reminded of it. Rich and powerful people in the past thought they did need these reminders because they had grown so important and influential that they might be tempted to believe they were immortal, so they included a skull in their portraits to symbolise their eventual return to dust. Modern man, who with the help of medicine and good sanitation has distanced himself from death much further than his ancestors ever managed, has come to the view that it's better to pretend death has nothing to do with him.

This may not be entirely fair, however. The skull in old portraits may have been an affectation, or a false modesty. Humans, in general, both in the past and in the present, have never conceptualised death very well.

The school I attended as a child was run by Jesuits. I particularly remember one of them; let's call him Father Müller. He was very old and very devout. Father Müller wasn't the most intellectually sophisticated priest in the school, but he was easily the most enthusiastic and least cynical of them all. When he finally had to approach death in a hospital ward, he was so overjoyed at the prospect of joining at last the celestial characters he had revered for so long, that he deliriously (in every sense of the word) started singing very loud chants and prayers, so loud and so persistently in fact that others in the ward weren't able to rest or sleep and Father Müller had to be isolated in a single room, where he continued to sing to his heart's content, until he died soon afterwards.

Father Müller's simple faith allowed him to look death in the eye when he realised his time had come. Others may be helped by a strong opiate, or by the brain dimming down its functions in anticipation of the final curtain. But until we get there, we need to pretend we are everlasting. Not others, of course; just me.

Vinicius de Moraes said in one of his poems that love "is not immortal, [...], but let it be infinite while it lasts". Similarly, we require life to be infinite while it lasts.

An American anthropologist called Ernest Becker[16] postulated an intriguing theory about our denial of death and how this denial may be the motor behind all sorts of human horrors, from the waging of wars to mental illness.

Becker was involved in the liberation of Nazi concentration camps while serving in the American army in his youth and this experience must have influenced his theories on how we see death (or don't see it, to be precise). He had been diagnosed with cancer before his influential book *The Denial of Death* was published, and died at the age of only 49. It is sadly ironic that the Pulitzer Prize he received for his book on death was awarded posthumously. He believed that depression is the result of the failure of one's "immortality project", which is reminiscent in a way of Polkinghorne's idea of depression being the result of the collapse of one's life narrative, but with a different focus. Becker maintained that we need this "immortality project" to remain intact in order to stay sane. We need to believe (not intellectually, of course, but emotionally) that we will never die, and when this belief is challenged by a glimpse of undeniable evidence, a state of melancholia ensues.

Becker also associated his idea of the immortality project with schizophrenia (less convincingly, in my view) and postulated that our immortality superhero powers help explain wars, acts of aggression, and all forms of intolerance. This is because each immortality project has the absolute need to

---

16 Oliver Burkeman comments about this author in his book *"The Antidote"*, in which he makes a very convincing case against positive thinking and how our modern obsession with all things positive can be in fact counterproductive.

prevail if it enters in conflict with another. Only by prevailing will it be able to continue to believe in itself.

Epicurus, the Greek philosopher who advocated a simple but pleasurable life, saw death denial as the source of much suffering. We would all be much happier if we just came to terms with the fact that one day we are going to die, and be done with it, according to Epicurus. Unfortunately, he experienced a very painful death himself, after suffering with kidney stones for 14 days, and yet he was apparently able to endure this ordeal quite cheerfully.

Epicurus' advice is unquestionably persuasive, but accepting the inevitability of death may not be that simple, as this denial is rooted very deeply in our brain's cognitive networks. The human brain's flat refusal to process any information concerning its future death has recently been demonstrated empirically by a very imaginative piece of research, conducted in Israel. In this experiment, volunteers were shown photos of people (including one of themselves) and words (half of them related to death, like "funeral", for example), while having their brain scanned, so they were able to observe the brain's reaction when a photo was shown following a death-related word. The scans proved that the volunteers' brains refused to associate death with their own photos. As far as our brain is concerned, death does happen, of course, but it happens *to others*. The author explains in an interview with an Israeli website that we are not meant to be fully aware of our own mortality, so if we get even a hint of it, perhaps through trauma, we feel profoundly distressed. I would add that such a hint can sometimes also result in a sense of bewilderment, as in the case of Alfred, my patient, who can't understand what's happening to him in old age.

"So, how are you?" I ask Alfred the next time we meet in clinic. I notice that he seems quite jovial today.

"Much better, thank you, doctor. You know how I was very worried about my health last time we spoke? Well, I had a frank chat with my GP and he explained how these things are not unusual when one is getting older."

I feel vaguely irritated by the fact that Alfred accepted the age argument from his GP, but not from me.

"These things happen with age," Alfred continues, "but they don't *mean* anything, you know, it's not as if I am *dying* or anything!"

"Of course you aren't. Nobody said you were dying."

"I thought you did."

Oh, well. I'm glad Alfred is feeling better, anyway.

CHAPTER 15

HOW HAPPY SHOULD I BE?

I am in clinic, listening to Martha, a very good looking middle-aged art gallery owner, impeccably dressed and well-spoken, the very embodiment of elegance. She has a Bipolar II disorder. This means that she has fluctuations in her mood that are not as pronounced as those found in a standard "Bipolar I" disorder, and yet these ups and downs may be more difficult to control with medication. Bipolar II patients rarely become so unwell that they need to be admitted to hospital (unlike those with a Bipolar I illness), but they tend to follow a very chronic course, and in a few unfortunate cases the patient may be almost constantly ill. Not infrequently, the reason for this chronicity is simply the fact that they are misdiagnosed as having a straight-forward depression (if there is such a thing) and given generic medication for this, which doesn't always help their specific disorder. Their periods of depression tend to be more frequent and longer than their periods of elation, so when one of these arrives, they are very welcome, even if they carry with them additional instability.

"The last few weeks have been great, I feel I'm back to who I really am, you know, after months of feeling down in the dumps," Martha starts.

Her facial expression is radiant, but she remains gracefully contained. She had tried to cancel the clinic appointment because she found it unnecessary to meet when she was feeling perfectly well in herself, but I convinced her over the phone to come and see me anyway.

"And I'm having ideas again. I am full of energy, I want to expand my business and I've been talking to someone I know in France about setting up a branch there, it's all very exciting. Also, I want to meet people again! In fact, I've met someone already; he's not perfect, but he makes me laugh, which is the most important thing. We are going to Peru together next week..."

"Well, that's great," I interrupt, "but you probably know what I'm going to say next."

"Yes, I do, but you're wrong, this is *me*, this is who I really am, the depressed woman you saw before wasn't me!"

Interesting thought. Which one is Martha? The morose, sad woman, who still manages somehow to do her hair every day and dress beautifully, but only out of a sense of duty, with no drive and no joy, or the bubbly, expansive Martha? Who is *normal* Martha?

"OK, I take that on board," I finally say, "but I'm just looking at this pragmatically. Let's try and reduce the chances of you going bankrupt, or of finding yourself stuck in a distant continent with the wrong sort of guy," I add, rather brutally. "How about calming things down just a notch with an additional tablet?" I ask her, knowing I don't really stand a chance.

Bipolar sufferers not infrequently place their normal self a little (or sometimes a lot) on the "high" side of their mood fluctuations. I don't blame them. I am not bipolar, and yet I also see any periods in my own life of relative distress, loss of confidence, or lack of *joie de vivre* as deviations from my "normal" self, even if statistically it remains to be seen whether my confident self happens more frequently than my sad one and would therefore define my "normal" character better. I wonder whether we all perhaps insist in chasing the upper segment of our mood variations, in the futile belief that we will be able to remain up there, where we think we belong, permanently.

How do we know a given mood is "normal"? Can we ever be sure a given mood isn't too high or too low, even if it "feels" normal? Perhaps my normal mood would be somebody else's low mood. We simply don't know.

When I was a young trainee I met a manic bipolar man who came to clinic accompanied by his wife. She was desperate and begged me to have her husband treated urgently and as vigorously as possible because he was becoming very unwell and impossible to live with. He was up all night doing D-I-Y and playing his guitar, she told me, and spent his days buying all sorts of expensive things he didn't need and getting into arguments with strangers. I obliged, but he was so high that it took a while to reach the necessary dose of tranquillisers that finally brought him down to what I regarded as a "normal" level. When I saw him again in clinic, he was finally calm. He wasn't groggy or "zombified"; he was just calm and composed, I thought. Pleased with myself, I looked at his wife expecting her to thank me with tears of gratitude in her eyes. She did have tears in her eyes, but they were tears of anger.

"He's not my husband. Look at him, he is all quiet and placid. The fizz and the spark have gone! What have you done to him?"

Happy and unhappy at the same time

If having different moods at different times wasn't enough (even to the point that we sometimes forget what a normal mood is), we also need to contend with the fact that a given moment in time often contains different and even contradictory emotions.

In an early 16th century painting, held at the Uffizi Gallery in Florence, Cupid complains to Venus that he has been stung by bees while stealing their honey. A few verses in Latin, written on the painting itself, remind us that in life there is no pleasure without pain.

One of the difficulties we encounter when we try to conceptualise the idea of happiness in our minds is the fact that a state of wellbeing is multi-faceted. In simple terms, it is often depicted as two intersecting dimensions: the vertical one representing arousal and the horizontal, "affect" (misery to the left and pleasure to the right). This results in four quadrants (going clockwise from the top): happy/excited, happy/serene, sad/ melancholy, and sad/agitated, plus all the in-between affective states, of course.

These two dimensions have their counterparts in music and, in fact, the different combinations of key and tempo also convey particular states of arousal and mood. A fast major key composition, such as the Italian national anthem, which is very jolly, or Mendelssohn's *Wedding March*, make us feel optimistic and energetic, whereas a slow major key song, like John Lennon's *Imagine*, or ABBA's *I have a dream*, will evoke calmness and serene, peaceful reflection. Slow minor key tunes may be sad and mournful, like in the case of Chopin's *Funeral March*, while traditional lullabies, typically in a minor key, will ease the tired child into a tranquil sleep. Fast minor key compositions are tense and dramatic and often express conflict in musical theatre, as in Judas' opening song in *Jesus Christ Superstar*, by Andrew Lloyd-Webber.

Someone called Christian FD Schubart, a German 18th century poet and composer (not to be confused with the famous Franz Schubert), took the trouble to describe, in wonderfully lyrical terms, the moods that each particular musical key conveyed. According to him, D minor expressed *"dejected womanhood which broods notions and illusions"*; B major announced "*wild passions, made up of the crudest colours*", while *"every fear, every hesitation of the shuddering heart breathes from the shocking E flat minor. If ghosts could speak, they would doubtless speak from this key"*.

If onc is feeling gloomy and morose, the thing to do might be to try to shake off the gloominess by stimulating the mind, like upping the tempo of a song in an effort to make it sound livelier, but this may also result in an increase in arousal and agitation, which will worsen the mood. The musical equivalent will be a very unhappy Judas singing a distressed and fast-paced anthem on top of a mountain. Conversely, if one attempts to calm down this agitation by simply tranquillising the mind, like slowing down the tempo in a song, the ensuing musical result, if mood remains unchanged, will be Chopin's *Funeral March*. The need to consider both dimensions is one of the main challenges a psychiatrist faces when treating an episode of depression.

Curiously, different sources have reported that hit songs are more likely to be written in a minor key nowadays, something almost unthinkable 10 or 20 years ago. Perhaps this is a sign that we live in a more contemplative era, although I somehow doubt it.

Some psychology scholars didn't want to stop at the affect and arousal model and identified instead countless other axes and emotional dimensions that affect our wellbeing, according to them. In any case, the fact that feeling good or bad is not the result of one single quantity of "wellness" allows for the existence of mixed and muddled emotional states.

I am a victim of a lifelong passion for old cars. Over the years, I have kept this passion under control, but not long ago

I succumbed to it and bought a very old sports car in less than perfect condition. Not having the time or the skill to look after it myself, I have to rely on expensive garages to do it for me, which fills me with vast quantities of anxiety when something goes wrong in the car, which happens more or less all the time. Today, I am driving it to the garage to have something (hopefully) fixed, but the traffic is heavy. I have developed a very keen ear for all the noises the car emits, which are very many, and their possible sinister significance, but what suddenly alarms me is much more immediate: the engine stalls and then restarts with a loud backfire. A few seconds later, I find myself in a traffic jam. I feel stressed and agitated, having to add this malfunction to the list of problems the car is accumulating. I then think of the metaphor a colleague of mine uses to explain what we call in psychiatry a Mixed Affective State, which is essentially a kind of depression that sometimes affects bipolar patients, such as Martha. This depression is accompanied by feelings of inner agitation and sometimes can be a perfect and paradoxical mixture of melancholia and elation, a kind of super-energised depression, or distressed mania, which is awfully difficult to endure and sufferers find equally difficult to describe. My colleague compares the agitation and tension one feels in a Mixed Affective State to a sports car revving its engine in a traffic jam. Well, I am feeling agitated and tense *and* I actually am in a sports car in a traffic jam.

Research has confirmed empirically that positive and negative emotions and affects can exist relatively independently of each other in the brain and that they can in fact happen simultaneously. We can feel excited and distressed, or loving and afraid, or moved by a bitter-sweet film. This is consistent with a model of messily intertwined and coexisting pleasure and pain, which fits our reality much better than the unachievable bliss the happiness industry is trying to sell us.

Our emotions are tangled and messy because they need to be that way. We react to a permanently changing environment, which demands feelings of alarm, frustration, disappointment and sadness, as well as joy, amusement and hope. The triggers for these sentiments frequently occur together and this is why the resulting emotions also occur together. It is simply impossible to disentangle the fear from the fun in the rollercoaster, or the sadness from the sweet nostalgia in a sentimental song, or the apprehension from the anticipation in an adventure. Love is notoriously contradictory:

> "*The pleasures of love are pains that become desirable, where sweetness and torment blend, and so love is voluntary insanity, infernal paradise, and celestial hell — in short, harmony of opposite yearnings, sorrowful laughter, soft diamond*". (Umberto Eco)

One cannot experience the positive emotions associated with riding the rollercoaster, listening to the sentimental song, planning an adventure, or experiencing love, without the negative ones at the same time. They are all part of the package. Even anger, that most unpleasant of emotions, may sometimes be the motor for a pleasant and simultaneous feeling of determination.

We know Nietzsche liked the whole idea of spicing up life with occasional doses of pain. He went as far as to hypothesise that pain and pleasure are two sides of the same coin:

> "*What if pleasure and displeasure were so tied together that whoever wanted to have as much as possible of one must also have as much as possible of the other — that whoever*

wanted to learn to "jubilate up to the heavens" would also have to be prepared for "depression unto death?"

If, as we have seen, key and tempo provide a useful analogy for mood and arousal, we can also see our mixed and sometimes contradictory emotions as a musical dissonance. As in music, these dissonances of feelings are very frequent and not necessarily ugly. Being able to combine emotions and live with the resulting dissonances seems to be a good thing that we learn to do better as we age. It is, in other words, a necessary life skill that helps us accept the imperfections of life and, indeed, our own imperfections.

We feel a mixed bag of feelings with positive, as well as with negative events, because life teaches us to take failures with resignation and successes with a pinch of salt. It is good for us too. Research has shown that those who are more proficient at mixing their feelings also seem to enjoy a better physical health than people who are inclined to have only one emotion at the time. This may be due to the fact that learning to take the good with the bad in life brings us a measure of serenity, which is always a good thing for our health.

Having said all this, it is important that we differentiate between the tangled emotions we all have much of the time and those in a Mixed Affective Disorder, represented by the sports car in the traffic jam. The first are normal and inevitable, probably even good; the second are pathological and need to be treated assertively.

The multi-dimensionality of emotional wellbeing is recognised in a treatment for depression that has emerged relatively recently, called rTMS[17]. Essentially, rTMS involves

17 It stands for "repetitive Transcranial Magnetic Stimulation", which is a bit of a mouthful.

stimulating certain parts of the brain with magnetic pulses delivered by a coil placed on the patient's head in order to either excite or damp down brain activity in that particular area. The patient is fully conscious during the treatment. She or he hears a clicking noise and feels a tapping sensation in the scalp with each magnetic pulse, typically delivered at a rate of between one and 10 pulses a second, depending on the protocol being used. When I treat my depressed patients with rTMS, I sometimes use different modalities in order to calm down the right-hand side of the frontal lobe with slowly delivered pulses and then stimulate the left one with a fast protocol. The right-hand side frontal part of the brain, which is the non-dominant one, is intimately involved in emotional processing, particularly in relation to negative emotions, whereas the dominant left-sided frontal lobe has mainly "executive" functions. By doing this, I inhibit the negative emotions on the right side first, and then increase positive motivation and impetus on the left side, in relatively independent interventions.

In a depressive illness – and probably in any state of general sadness, pathological or otherwise – the negative emotions are too prominent and displace the weak positive ones, unbalancing the normal emotional blend.

Having established that we are not sure what a normal mood is, and that in any case such normal mood must be made up of a messy mixture of feelings, we need to relativise the concept even further by accepting that wellbeing is...well, *relative*. This is because rewards only make us happy when they exceed our expectations, as research has shown. So the millionaire who, after a hard day at work, expects to be able to sit at the terrace of his luxurious villa overlooking Lake Garda and sip a gin and tonic brought to him by his butler, while admiring the sunset, will be only moderately happy if this is what actually happens that evening. Nothing will have exceeded his expectations.

Conversely, a defect in this idyllic but expected scene – an overcast sky, the gin and tonic a tad warm, or intrusive music from a party in a neighbouring palazzo – will make him feel quite unhappy.

Happiness is elusive indeed.

Martha did go to Peru, where she realised that her companion wasn't that much fun to be with after all and her mood started to deteriorate again. She had to endure the beginning of a new episode of depression away from home and with a man beside her who was effectively a stranger and, in her own words, "a bit of a git, actually". Back in the clinic, we review the situation.

"I'm glad to be back home, if nothing else."

I don't have the desire, or even the right, to say "I told you so". It would be insensitive, but more importantly, I am wrong often enough not to gloat when I happen to be right.

"Nothing awful has happened and now I seem to be back to my usual depression, but there is something important I need to ask you, and it's this: do I need to accept that being depressed is my new *normal*? Perhaps it isn't even new; perhaps I was also sad much of the time even before I started having mood swings and I've forgotten? I was happy when I met Roberto and he convinced me to visit Peru with him. *Why couldn't that happiness be normal?*"

Uncharacteristically, I say nothing for a few seconds, simply because I don't know what to say. I then start talking, but only to try to reassure her with some anodyne, insipid waffle about the importance of mood stability, etc. In essence however, I don't have a satisfactory answer to her question. I have now written a whole book on why we can't be happy, but deep down I still feel somewhat puzzled (is this the right word? "Frustrated", or even "angry" might be better) that Nature, in all her genius, couldn't work out a way in which her creatures wouldn't have to suffer during their brief time on this planet.

I do know the reasons why Martha can't be happy, even if we disregard her bipolar disorder, but I don't know why Nature has programmed things to be this way. All right, I *also* know why Nature has programmed things to be this way; what I don't understand lies at a deeper level, beneath evolution itself. What I don't understand, *really*, is the reason why life must necessarily be precarious and competitive. This precariousness is what underpins Nature's obsession with survival and reproduction, which is the origin of all our unhappiness. A different Nature could have chosen to design things differently. So, no, deep down I don't really know the answer to Martha's question.

There, I've said it.

CHAPTER 16

HELP YOURSELF TO LASHINGS OF HAPPINESS

In 1859, a Scottish author called Samuel Smiles, who had been brought up in a large and strict Presbyterian family, published a book entitled *"Self-Help; with Illustrations of Character and Conduct"*. Smiles was unable to interest a publisher, so he took the very congruent decision to help himself and self-published it. It was an immediate sensation. Smiles' book popularised the idea of the deserving and the undeserving poor, which found an echo in conservative politics over a century later. More importantly, *"Self-help"* was the book that named a new genre. Its aim was to encourage the poor to educate and better themselves in order to improve their living conditions and even become gentlemen – a revolutionary idea at the time.

Émile Coué de la Châtaigneraie was another precursor of the positive thinking movement. A French chemist of the late 19th century, he became known for the very enthusiastic way in which he described the effectiveness of the remedies he sold to his clients, increasing in this way the power of the placebo effect of the drug. He must have realised that his call was in the field of psychology and not as an apothecary, so he started training in hypnosis in 1901 and later opened a clinic at Nancy, in which he offered his many patients a method of healing and self-improvement based on "autosuggestion". This involved the frequent repetition of the formula, *"Every day, in every way, I'm getting better and better"*. It isn't very clear how his clients dealt with any objective evidence to the contrary, which surely must have arisen quite frequently.

However, it was Norman Vincent Peale's *"The Power of Positive Thinking"* that revolutionised the self-help market and helped it evolve into its modern form. It was published in 1952, almost a century after Smiles' book, and 30 years after Coué's own book on his method of autosuggestion.

Peale was an American pastor with no training in psychology, who invented and popularised the concept of positive thinking. He could easily be described as a reactionary, but he was also a very good communicator and creative thinker, who managed to combine positive thinking with religion and even with psychoanalysis, with the help of a colleague called Smiley Blanton[18], with whom he opened a clinic. He was favoured by Republican presidents, including Richard Nixon, who was a personal friend, and Donald Trump, who has cited Peale's *"The Power of Positive Thinking"* to highlight the role that faith has played in his life. Peale once described Trump as "kindly and courteous" with "a streak of honest humility", according to the *Washington Post*, which makes one wonder if he was perhaps accidentally thinking of a different person when he said it. Peale campaigned against the election of JF Kennedy during the 1960 presidential election, on the grounds that the election of a Catholic president would threaten American culture. He may have had a very positive mind, but it certainly wasn't a very open one.

Since Peale, the self-help industry has grown to become a monster that Smiles wouldn't have been able to recognise. It is

18 Smiley Blanton had been a patient of Sigmund Freud. It is mildly amusing that among the crucial figures in the early history of self-help and positive thinking one was called Smiles and another Smiley.

now worth $11billion a year, according to Forbes, and three million self-help books are sold in the UK alone in a year.

The self-help genre is not a homogeneous beast, however. It is in fact ironic how self-help books on happiness and those on how to make it big in life are lumped together in the same bookshop shelves, given that many of the former tell us that caring too much about the latter is the main obstacle to happiness.

Self-help books teach us how to become more assertive and confident, fulfil our career ambitions, climb the greasy pole in the workplace and reach a better social status. They will assist us in our efforts to lose weight and turn into a more attractive, influential and admired person. They are designed, in short, to help us build a more desirable version of ourselves.

Unfortunately, if you are counting on this new and improved *you* making you happy, you'll be disappointed. This is because self-improvement projects are simply incompatible with every philosophical approach to happiness we have considered in this book, all of which demand that we detach ourselves from desire. Self-improvement projects involve a "libidinal" investment (a desire, in other words) from its protagonist, arguably of a narcissistic nature. The slim and confident guy, who knows how to chat up women successfully, make himself indispensable at work and then demand a raise, or even become a thriving entrepreneur, is unlikely to emerge from the advice contained in the books and, in any case, he is too busy striving, desiring and competing to be able to take a step back and be happy.

The pursuit of personal goals and achievements (and in addition to status, sexual conquests and wealth, I would also include here collecting exciting life experiences and even feats of physical fitness) is driven by desire. The belief underpinning this libidinal impetus is that the acquisition of all these attributes will help us put together the person we want to become. Inevitably however, this turns into a gluttonous self-building enterprise, reminiscent of Ernest Becker's futile "immortality project". It is very much about first desiring and then struggling to become a certain person we are not, the very opposite of what one is supposed to do in order to reach a state of serene contentment.

Physical exercise provides a good illustration of the values attached to the immortality and self-building projects. It is postulated as a universally "good" thing and we are often reminded by doctors and even by the government that we should exercise more. Youth and vigour are emphasised by physical fitness, making it a very desirable feature. And yet, when I see people jogging along in the street, they don't look particularly happy to me. They look tense and fatigued, and seem reluctant to change course to avoid colliding with others, perhaps because doing so would affect their lap time. Running is no longer fun. It has become a stressful personal improvement pursuit.

Despite the fact that the self-improvement genre was popularised by a cleric, books in this genre don't appear to concern themselves with altruism very much. This would be of course a very legitimate means of building a better version of ourselves, while avoiding the selfish and narcissistic aspects of personal brand building. The very name of the self-help genre indicates that it is the reader – and nobody else – who will be the recipient of the help.

As we have seen, a variety of thinkers have found that it is pointless to chase happiness itself, but as Michael Foley notes in his book *"The Age of Absurdity"*, we can still chase certain surrogates of happiness, such as money, fun, and cheerfulness. This is what the self-building branch of the optimism industry specialises on and it resonates with the increasingly prevalent idea in our culture that life is about living it to the full, consuming as much of it as we possibly can while we are here. Ticking every item in a long and ambitious bucket list is the only thing that matters. Meanwhile, the more inspirational gurus that push a direct route to happiness, disregarding its shallow proxies, promote a systematic, unremitting, unquestioning and indefatigable optimism. Personally, I have to say that the mere thought of having to feel positive about everything all the time makes me feel very tired. Mandatory optimism seems to me to be more of a task than a relief from suffering.

A striking feature of all these optimistic manuals, blogs and now even smart phone apps (which at the time of writing these lines include such catchy upbeat names as *"happify"*, *"Yolify"*, or even *"SuperBetter"*), is the apparent ease with which a state of fulfilment and personal satisfaction can be reached following their instructions. In some cases, the method to be followed may involve no more than 10 easy steps, which are far fewer than the steps needed to assemble an IKEA wardrobe. Unfortunately, this apparent simplicity implies that there must be something fundamentally wrong with those who fail in their attempts to be happy, adding to their sense of failure.

Certain websites that specialise in positive thinking explain that the difference between "billionaires" and the rest of us is that the former persevere in their efforts to make it big. They don't give up as easily as the rest of us gloomy mortals because they think positively. Never mind the obvious obstacles to become a billionaire, they are all perfectly surmountable, it seems, although I strongly suspect the writers of such websites aren't billionaires themselves. Negative thinking is the main reason why most start-ups fail, they say. That's the problem with the world, we are all just too damn defeatist, it seems.

I wonder however what would happen if a positive thinker had to compete with a bunch of other positive thinkers, if none of them would ever give up.

In reality, as we saw at the beginning of the book, accepting defeat has an adaptive function because persevering in the face of very unfavourable or impossible odds will be in the long run much more punishing than accepting reality.

Positive thinkers' advice on how to become rich and successful is almost amusing, but it gets more sinister when the positive thinking sages urge their readers to cure their own mental health problems with the help of a little positive magic dust.

Mr D is the quintessential sensible middle class, middle-aged Englishman. Austere and measured, he would never overstate a sentiment or draw attention to himself without cause. He also feels it is his absolute duty to try to face adversity alone and without bothering others, if possible. Mr D became quite depressed shortly after his retirement. Being very much a doer, he couldn't adjust to a sedentary life with no clear role and purpose after a long career as a surgeon, and being a thinker as well as a doer, he was determined to think his way out of his depression.

"I should be able to snap out of this vicious circle with the help of some positive thinking," he explained the first time we met. "I've been reading on this and I think I can do it. Well, I can't at the moment because I don't seem to be able to concentrate or govern my mind; my thoughts are all over the place. But if I persist, I should be able to crack it. The trouble is that my thoughts are racing all the time and they are all horrible. It's going to be very hard work to turn them into positive ones instead. It's torture, really."

He looks very tense as he says this. He looks in fact, tortured, as he says. This is because he has an agitated depression (remember the sports car revving its engine in a traffic jam, or the fast tempo and minor key musical combination). In an agitated depression, the sufferer gets stuck in an accelerated melancholia, which can be very dangerous. Doctors make bad patients, as everybody knows, and Mr D is a good example of this. He won't accept medication.

Mr D didn't snap out of it. Something did snap, but it wasn't his depression. It was instead the rope that he tied to a ceiling beam in his garage. Luckily, the rope was a little rotten in places, as he explained later. Also luckily, Mr D recovered fully, with the help of intensive treatment. The treatment package didn't include any self-help recipes.

"I am a surgeon, I should have known better,"

says Mr D when we met in clinic again a couple of months after the episode in the garage. I sense he is not referring to the consequences of his treatment refusal.

"What do you mean?"

"My weight is 95 kg and the rope I used was too thin and had been kept in a damp garage for years. A surgeon like me should have realised that was never going to work. That's how ill I was; I couldn't even judge the situation properly."

Needing to explain that the illness had clouded his ability to judge the type of rope needed for the job is consistent with Mr D's technically minded and manly character. He is however very pleased to be alive.

"My wife and I are going to spend the winter in the South of France and I'm really looking forward to that. We have rented a cottage in the same town where we first met 35 years ago."

After a pause, he adds in a reflective tone:

"You were right, you know; I couldn't even kill myself, so I could hardly have helped myself out of my depression with this self-help positive thinking nonsense."

"I wouldn't say that using the wrong rope was a failure," I reply. "You should be more compassionate with yourself. It was very fortunate."

"I wasn't so much thinking of the rope; what I mean is that my weight was a major factor. I must have put on 10 kilos, at least, in as many years, no wonder the rope snapped. This has made me realise that I should lose weight pronto. At our age one can't be too careful!"

(Steady, I'm younger than you!) I think this, but I don't say it. He continues:

"You wouldn't know of a good self-help dieting book, would you?"

I think he's joking, but I'm not sure. Surgeons have a weird sense of humour.

CHAPTER 17

DIAGNOSIS

Julio is a narcissist. He is many other things too, but he is certainly a narcissist.

Today, the very pleasant receptionist hands me over my clinic list and my heart sinks when I see Julio's name at the top, not because I personally dislike him, but because I know the consultation will be too long and then my whole clinic will be running late.

I say I don't dislike Julio, which is strange, given that he is a narcissist. There are two reasons for this. The first is that in other respects, Julio is a complex, intelligent and stimulating person. He used to work as a butcher until his worsening mental health problems forced him to stop not long ago, still in his forties and still single. Julio is very well educated, so I see his blue collar occupation not as a strange dissonance, but as a way of avoiding competition in arenas that might have challenged his narcissism. The second reason is that, unlike many other narcissists, he has a very obvious vulnerable side that elicits a feeling of compassion in me. His weaknesses are very near the surface, so one quickly realises that the reason why he has persuaded himself that he is better than others is that he can't be like others, which, deep down, is what he would really like, I believe. His arrogance and apparent self-sufficiency are necessary complements to his inability to engage with others cooperatively.

Julio is depressed.

"I think I know what's making me depressed. I think the reason is that I am so creative and so receptive to the suffering of others. Others go through life not noticing these things, but *I* do. Too much, in fact."

"Well, I see how that could be a problem."

I say this half-heartedly, not really wanting the conversation to go down that road.

"My life is shit because I don't fit, and the irony is that I don't fit because I'm *better*. I can't work because colleagues always resent my superior abilities, and I can't have a partner because women seem to think that my sophistication and intelligence make me effeminate."

"I see; I think we should focus on your depression..."

"And I have a big personality. I feel that sometimes in life it's better to go unnoticed, but I can't, because wherever I am, people take notice of me, it's inevitable."

"A heavy cross to bear, I'm sure."

"So, I've been thinking, I think I have what you call a 'personality disorder', yes, I think I may have one of those."

Julio reflects for a few seconds, making me feel intrigued.

"But only in the sense that I have *too much* personality. I suffer because I carry a very big person in me. You see what I mean, doctor?"

Julio wants a diagnosis that will give some meaning to his unhappiness and that will suit the inflated idea he has of himself. He already has two diagnoses (Depressive Illness and Narcissistic Personality Disorder), which this conversation suggests we may have to revise and negotiate together. In medicine, we provide diagnoses quite liberally and tend to see anything that either deviates from the norm or produces any measure of distress as pathological. This is arguably unhelpful, as it denies the inevitability of suffering in human life and fosters feelings of inadequacy among those who are in pain.

The World Health Organisation defines health, very ambitiously, as a "state of complete physical, mental, and social well-being, and not merely the absence of disease or infirmity." This definition makes it very clear that anything less than complete mental well-being is unhealthy. It is, in other words, pathological, and therefore deserves to be treated, even if that necessitates labelling the unhappy as pathological and medicalising them. The irony is that a great proportion of actual mental illness, of the kind that most certainly deserves a diagnosis, goes unidentified and untreated, despite the medicalisation of unhappiness at the opposite end of the spectrum. Research has shown that a very significant percentage of all genuine depressions are never diagnosed or treated.

Medicine medicalises. In 1851, a Louisiana doctor called Samuel A. Cartwright proposed a diagnosis in an article published in the New Orleans Medical and Surgical Journal, which he coined as *"Drapetomania"*. This diagnosis was to be applied to slaves who ran away, which Cartwright considered an obviously pathological behaviour. Even now, you will be able to find in the latest edition of the International Classification of Diseases the appropriate diagnostic code for someone who picks his nose too enthusiastically and another for a person who doesn't get on with his mother-in-law[19]. If nose picking, a tense relationship with an in-law, and even running away from slavery have all been medicalised, it is hardly surprising that unhappiness has entered the medicine books too (despite Richard Bentall's good-humoured effort to describe happiness

19 The ICD-10 diagnostic codes for these issues are F98.8 and Z63.1 respectively.

– its opposite – as a diagnosable disorder, on which we commented earlier in the book).

When even a normal bereavement reaction to the loss of a loved one became diagnosable a few years ago, experts argued that giving a diagnosis of depression to a distressed person who had suffered a loss "substituted a superficial medical ritual for deep and time-honoured cultural ones". The WHO's dystopic idea of a healthy world seems to require the eradication of pain from life, by banishing unpleasant emotions and labelling them as pathological and medically treatable.

Medicalising unhappiness poses two major problems. The first is that it is based on a fallacy because, as we have already established, pain is one of the intrinsic components of life and part of its very fabric. The second problem is that it creates an expectation that any kind of psychological suffering can be successfully treated, which is simply not true.

Attaching diagnostic codes to unhappiness is a way of rejecting it as something alien that doesn't really belong to us. This allows us to see our unhappiness as a disorder we have caught and not as something that we own. It is a bit like externalising evil impulses by attributing them to the Devil. Convenient, but untrue.

Julio, in contrast, embraces his negative emotions because he feels they help define him as a person. He doesn't reject them, as many of us try to do, because feeling sad – he believes – is the direct consequence of his extraordinary and superior personal characteristics, which the sadness confirms. His suffering is therefore the inevitable burden that he hopes to mitigate, but certainly not cure.

"There is one thing I want to discuss, doctor, it's about my diagnosis."

This is how Julio opens the conversation when we meet again in clinic. I think I know where this is going. I haven't shared my thoughts about his narcissism with him because I know they would hurt him, so he must be referring to his depression, a diagnosis that Julio probably finds too dry and too generic. I am right, as it turns out.

"Depression!"

He starts enigmatically, and then continues after a dramatic pause:

"Everybody is depressed, so saying that I am depressed doesn't explain my issues, or what I am about. I bet most people in your clinic today have the same diagnosis, and yet I'm sure you'll agree they aren't like me."

"I totally agree, we are all different."

"You know what I mean, don't be disingenuous, doctor. The word 'depression' doesn't even start to describe the complexities of my psychological processes. I experience deep and intricate existential struggles within me, as you well know. Others may be just low in mood. Not me."

My clinic is going to run late yet again.

"What diagnosis do you think would suit you better?" I say, in an effort to placate Julio.

"How about *Psychogenic* Depression?"

Oh dear, I can't really remember what that is, but he has clearly looked it up and knows what it is. This, I should explain, shouldn't be too surprising. Each standard diagnosis has multiple equivalents that have become obsolete over the years. I wonder where he found this one. He must have been looking hard. I am pressed for time so I am about to concede his desired diagnosis regardless, when he adds:

"Well, that's in Axis I, of course. For Axis II, I thought you could say I have a *Character Neurosis not otherwise specified*, ICD code F60.9. As for Axes III to V..."

"Character Neurosis can mean almost anything."

I say this impulsively and regretting it immediately because I really, *really*, don't want to enter into a deep discussion about Julio's diagnoses, which would undoubtedly be long and futile.

"Yes, I have to agree there," Julio says in a reflective voice, to my surprise.

"I think it needs to be more specific. You know, doctor, on reflection, I think I may have a *Narcissistic Personality Disorder*. Would you agree?"

CHAPTER 18

POSITIVE CONCLUSION (PARADOXICALLY)

Philosophical and ethical recipes for happiness are all very good and legitimate, as long as we bear in mind the metaphor of the fire in the Arctic: the fire will help a little, but won't alter the prevalent Arctic climate. Similarly, there is no doubt that certain attitudes, such as altruism, or escaping from a never ending cycle of desire and consumption, will help us make the best out of life in terms of wellbeing (or happiness, if you really want to use that word), but like the cold in the Arctic, our inevitably mixed emotions will remain the prevalent climate in our mind, regardless.

I find it more difficult to recommend "positive thinking" as a good way of approaching the challenges we encounter in life. Positive thinking is a self-explanatory and intellectually very simple idea, which, as we saw, seems to be primarily designed to pursue goals that have little to do with happiness. Even more importantly, it probably doesn't work that well, anyway. An American psychologist called Gabriele Oettingen once studied a set of obese women who had enrolled in a weight reduction programme and found that the more positively these women imagined their outcome, the fewer pounds they lost. Oettingen believes that thinking positively may paradoxically drain the energy we need to achieve our goals. The positive fantasy makes us feel good, which is what matters at the end of the day, so we don't bother doing anything about the objective itself.

It is perhaps a little unfair to single out positive thinking at the end of the book as a prominent example of an ineffective happiness-seeking strategy because, at the end of the day and regardless of our philosophical beliefs, we are all bound to stumble eventually on the same obstacle: our DNA doesn't know how to do happiness. This is frustrating because it does know how to do thousands of other less important things.

Happiness is not a natural state; it is quite simply a myth, a ghost, an abstract idea humans made up and then started chasing as if it were real. But it isn't, and the sooner we accept this fact, the better.

So, to sum up:

- Nature and evolution couldn't care less about our happiness and, in fact, they have a vested interest in making sure we remain on our toes, forever anxious and unsatisfied.
- Money helps, but not that much.
- Detachment and renunciation may also help, but they aren't much fun.
- Moralistic preachers tell us it is all our fault, but it isn't, really. It is Nature's fault.
- Certain personality types find it even more difficult to be happy than others.
- There is no secret door to eventual happiness through suffering. We sort of knew that already, but we checked, just in case.
- There is no respite to be found in our dreams. Not in the dreams we have in our sleep, anyway.
- There is no such thing as a happy pill.
- If we found a way to make our brain feel happy artificially, our species would die out.
- We seem to have mislaid paradise.

- We leak innocence capital the older we get.
- Our lives don't go anywhere in particular.
- Our brain is wired to have mixed, messy and coexisting emotions.
- Self-help and positive thinking aren't all they are cracked up to be.
- We can diagnose unhappiness, but we cannot cure it with tablets or with a scalpel.

This book postulates that there is no such thing as happiness, which could easily be interpreted as a totally negative message. But there is a crucial silver lining in this apparently black cloud: understanding why our biological self will never manage to be happy and rejecting the idea of happiness as an achievable goal will liberate us from its oppressive demands.

Our intermittent and fluctuating unhappiness does not really represent a personal failure. It is not a shortcoming that demands urgent repair, as the happiness gurus would have it. Far from it. Our mixed, fluctuating, untidy, and not always pleasant emotions are what make us human. And that's surely something to be proud of.

Rafa Euba,
London, 2020

BIBLIOGRAPHY

The fourteen happy days of the Caliph

All about Philosophy. Abd-ar-Rahman III – His Pursuits. https://www.allaboutphilosophy.org/abd-ar-rahman-iii.htm

The Encyclopaedia Britannica. Abd al-Rahmān III, Umayyad caliph. https://www.britannica.com/biography/Abd-al-Rahman-III

Euba R, 2019. Happy days – Psychiatry in history. The British Journal of Psychiatry; 214(06):328.

Vallejo-Nájera JA, 1992 (first published 1989). Locos Egregios. Planeta.

Maslow, AH, 1970. Motivation and personality. New York: Harper & Row.

Frank RH, 2007. The Economic Naturalist. London: Virgin Books.

Evolution

Charles Darwin, 2004 (first published in 1859). The Origin of Species. Castle Books.

Círculo de Poesía. Revista electrónica de literatura. Poemas de Vinicius de Moraes. https://circulodepoesia.com/2013/05/poemas-de-vinicius-de-moraes/

Boylan M, 2006. Hippocrates. Internet Encyclopedia of Philosophy. https://www.iep.utm.edu/hippocra/

Dunea, G, 2007. "The Anatomy of Melancholy". British Medical Journal. 335: 351.2–351. doi:10.1136/bmj.39301.684363.59.

Stearns PN. The History of Happiness. Harvard Business Review, January–February 2012 Issue.

The Times. Commercial Depression and Anxiety. 8th March 1880. Page 13.

Wagner-Egger P et al., 2018. Creationism and conspiracism share a common teleological bias. Current Biology. 28:847-870. 10.1016/j.cub.2018.06.072.

Gabbatiss J. Scientists discover the reason people believe in conspiracy theories. The Independent, 20 August 2018. https://www.independent.co.uk/news/science/conspiracy-theories-creationism-psychology-911-moon-landing-fake-a8499511.html

Burkhardt, RW Jr., 1970. Lamarck, evolution, and the politics of science. Journal of the History of Biology 3: 275–298. doi:10.1007/bf00137355.

Marcaggi G and Guénolé F, 2018. Freudarwin: Evolutionary Thinking as a Root of Psychoanalysis. Front Psychol. 9: 892. doi: 10.3389/fpsyg.2018.00892

Andrews PW and Thompson JA, 2009. The bright side of being blue: depression as an adaptation for analyzing complex problems. Psychological Review, 116, 620–654.

Nesse RM, 2000. Is Depression an Adaptation? Archives of General Psychiatry, 57, 14–20.

Watson PJ and Andrews PW, 2002. Toward a revised evolutionary adaptationist analysis of depression: the social navigation hypothesis. Journal of Affective Disorders, 72, 1-14.

Bentall RP, 1992. A proposal to classify happiness as a psychiatric disorder. Journal of Medical Ethics, 18, 94-98.

Goldberg V. In search of Diana of Ephesus. New York Times, Aug. 21, 1994. https://www.nytimes.com › 1994/08/21 › arts › in-search-of-diana-of-ephesus

Hazard P, 1964. The European Mind, 1680-1715. Penguin Books.

Moore G, 2002. Reappraising Dickens's 'Noble Savage'. Dickensian, 98:236-243.

Dawkins R, 2006. The Blind Watchmaker: Why the Evidence of Evolution Reveals a Universe Without Design. Penguin.

Personality

Cervantes M, 2008 (first published 1605). Don Quijote de la Mancha. Punto de Lectura.

Hans and Sybil Eysenck. https://www.hanseysenck.co.uk/home.html

Furnham A and Brewin CR, 1990. Personality and happiness. Personality and Individual Differences, 11:1093-1096.

Haller CS and Courvoisier, DS, 2010. Personality and thinking style in different creative domains. Psychology of Aesthetics, Creativity, and the Arts, 4:149–160. https://doi.org/10.1037/a0017084

Maslow AH, 1964. Religions, values, and peak experiences. London: Penguin.

Singer L,1998. Ideology and ethics. The perversion of German psychiatrists' ethics by the ideology of national socialism. European Psychiatry, 13, Supp 3:87s-92s.

Coughlan S. Narcissists 'horrible people but happy'. BBC News, 29 October 2019.

Kaufman SB. Can Intelligence Buy You Happiness? Scientific American, 16 December 2018.

Raina M and Bakhshi A, 2013. Emotional Intelligence Predicts Eudaimonic Well Being. IOSR Journal of Humanities and Social Science,11:42-47.

Goleman D, 2006. Emotional Intelligence: Why It Can Matter More Than IQ. Bantam.

Joseph, DL and Newman DA, 2010. Emotional intelligence: An integrative meta-analysis and cascading model. Journal of Applied Psychology, 95:54–78. https://doi.org/10.1037/a0017286

April K et al., 2012. Impact of Locus of Control Expectancy on Level of Well-Being. Review of European Studies, 4:124-137.

The Biology of Unhappiness

Olds J and Milner P, 1954. Positive reinforcement produced by electrical stimulation of septal area and other regions of rat brain. J. Comp. Physiol. Psychol. 47: 419–427. doi:10.1037/h0058775

Sternbach LH, 1972. The discovery of Librium. Agents Actions, 2:193-6. doi: 10.1007/BF01965860

Blakemore C, 1988. The Mind Machine. BBC Books.

Brady MP. Keys to Diagnosing Broken Heart Syndrome (Takotsubo Cardiomyopathy). Medscape, 29 October 2019. https://reference.medscape.com/slideshow/broken-heart-syndrome-6012067

Queensland Brain Institute. The limbic system. The University of Queensland. https://qbi.uq.edu.au/brain/brain-anatomy/limbic-system

Forster GL at al. The Amygdala - A Discrete Multitasking Manager. The Role of the Amygdala in Anxiety Disorders. IntechOpen, 19 December 2012. DOI: 10.5772/50323. www.intechopen.com/books/the-amygdala-a-discrete-multitasking-manager/the-role-of-the-amygdala-in-anxiety-disorders

Kanai R et al, 2011. Political Orientations Are Correlated with Brain Structure in Young Adults. Current Biology, 21:677-680. DOI:https://doi.org/10.1016/j.cub.2011.03.017

Shorter E, 1997. A history of psychiatry. From the era of the asylum to the age of Prozac. New York: John Wiley and Sons.

Nijensohn DE et al, 2012. New Evidence of Prefrontal Lobotomy in the Last Months of the Illness of Eva Perón. World Neurosurgery, 77:583-590 https://doi.org/10.1016/j.wneu.2011.02.036

Drugs and Happy Pills

Abidemi Idowu Otaiku. Did René Descartes Have Exploding Head Syndrome? Journal of Clinical Sleep Medicine, Vol 14. Published Online: April 15, 2018 https://doi.org/10.5664/jcsm.7068

Gearhart S. Phineas Gage, American railroad foreman. Encyclopaedia Britannica. https://www.britannica.com/biography/Phineas-Gage

Kramer P, 1993. Listening to Prozac. New York City: Viking.

Klerman, GL, 1972. Psychotropic hedonism vs. pharmacological Calvinism. Hastings Cent Rep, 2:1–3.

Moncrieff J and Kirsch I. Efficacy of antidepressants in adults. BMJ 2005, 331:155-157. doi: https://doi.org/10.1136/bmj.331.7509.155

Morgan CJ and Curran HVm 2012. Independent Scientific Committee on Drugs. Ketamine use: a review. Addiction, 107:27-38. doi: 10.1111/j.1360-0443.2011.03576.x.

Baumeister D, Tracy D et al, 2014. Classical hallucinogens as antidepressants? A review of pharmacodynamics and putative clinical roles Ther Adv Psychopharmacol, 4: 156–169. doi: 10.1177/2045125314527985

Huxley A, 1977. Doors of Perception. Heaven & Hell. London: HarperCollins.

Huxley A, 1998 (first published in 1932). A Brave New World. Harper Perennial / Perennial Classics.

Nozick R, 1974. Anarchy, State, and Utopia. New York: Basic Books.

Food and Sex

Cross FL, 1966. The Oxford Dictionary of the Christian Church. Oxford University Press.
Shipley O, 1875. A Theory About Sin: In Relation to Some Facts of Daily Life. Books.google.uk
Snowdon C. Revealed: Public Health England's cosy love-in with the anti-alcohol lobby. Spectator Health, 27 April 2017.
Bratman S and Knight D, 2000. Health Food Junkies: Overcoming the Obsession with Healthful Eating. New York: Broadway Books.
Mill JS,2002. The Basic Writings Of John Stuart Mill: On Liberty, The Subjection of Women and Utilitarianism. Random House.
Klausen JC, 2016. Violence and Epistemology J. S. Mill's Indians after the "Mutiny". Political Research Quarterly, 69: 96–107. doi:10.1177/1065912915623379
UCL. Auto-Icon. https://www.ucl.ac.uk/bentham-project/who-was-jeremy-bentham/auto-icon
Duignan B. What Is Jeremy Bentham's "Auto-Icon"? Encyclopaedia Britannica. https://www.britannica.com/story/what-is-jeremy-benthams-auto-icon
Driver J, 2009. The History of Utilitarianism. Stanford Encyclopedia of Philosophy. https://plato.stanford.edu/entries/utilitarianism-history/
Dupré B, 2007. 50 philosophy ideas you really need to know. London: Quercus.
Grafton A, Most GW, Settis S, 2010. The Classical Tradition. Harvard University Press.
The Editors of the Encyclopedia Britannica. Sybaris. https://www.britannica.com/place/Sybaris
Love Actually, 2003. Written and directed by Richard Curtis. StudioCanal, Working Title Films, DNA Films.

Wealth does make you happy after all (to a point)

George Bernard Shaw. The Collected Works of Bernard Shaw. PergamonMedia. Kindle Edition.

Easterlin R. The science of happiness can trump GDP as a guide for policy. The Conversation, 13 April, 2016. https://theconversation.com/the-science-of-happiness-can-trump-gdp-as-a-guide-for-policy-57004

Clark AE et al., 2008. Relative Income, Happiness, and Utility: An Explanation for the Easterlin Paradox and Other Puzzles. Journal of Economic Literature, 46: 95-144. DOI: 10.1257/jel.46.1.95

Pinsker J. The Reason Many Ultrarich People Aren't Satisfied With Their Wealth. The Atlantic, 4 December 2018. https://www.theatlantic.com/family/archive/2018/12/rich-people-happy-money/577231/

Donnelly E et al., 2018. The Amount and Source of Millionaires' Wealth (Moderately) Predicts Their Happiness. Personality and Social Psychology Bulletin 44:684–699.

The Editors of Encyclopaedia Britannica. Diogenes, Greek philosopher. https://www.britannica.com/biography/Diogenes-Greek-philosopher

IEP. Diogenes of Sinope (c. 404-323 B.C.E.). https://www.iep.utm.edu/diogsino/

Helliwell et al, eds. World Happiness Report 2020. New York: Sustainable Development Solutions Network. https://happiness-report.s3.amazonaws.com/2020/WHR20.pdf

Gallup 2019 Global Emotions Report. https://www.gallup.com/analytics/248906/gallup-global-emotions-report-2019.aspx

Arora V. Bhutan's Human Rights Record Defies 'Happiness' Claim. The Diplomat, 25 April 2014.

Locke J, 1753. An Essay concerning Human Understanding. The fourteenth edition. books.google.co.uk

The Pursuit of Happyness, 2006. Directed by Gabriele Muccino. Based on The Pursuit of Happyness by Chris Gardner and Quincy Troupe. Columbia Pictures.

Preachers say it's our fault

Matthieu Ricard. https://www.matthieuricard.org/en/

Kral TRA et al., 2018. Impact of short- and long-term mindfulness meditation training on amygdala reactivity to emotional stimuli. NeuroImage, 181:301-313.

Iyer P. Does California's commitment to happiness end up leaving us bereft? Los Angeles Times, 28 April 2019.

Mookerjeea R and Beronb K, 2005. Gender, religion and happiness. The Journal of Socio-Economics, 34:674-685.

Berthold A and Ruch W, 2014. Satisfaction with life and character strengths of non-religious and religious people: it's practicing one's religion that makes the difference. Frontiers in Psychology, 5:876.

Rolland R,1929. Beethoven the Creator. Harper & Brothers.

Papova M. The Joy of Suffering Overcome: Young Beethoven's Stirring Letter to His Brothers About the Loneliness of Living with Deafness and How Music Saved His Life. Brain Pickings. https://www.brainpickings.org/2017/02/08/beethoven-romain-rolland-letters/

Nietzsche F, 1968. The Will to Power. Random House.

Cybulska, EM, 2000. The madness of Nietzsche: a misdiagnosis of the millennium? Hospital Medicine. 61: 571–75.

Owen AM, 2011. The Monte Carlo fallacy. Medical Journal of Australia 2011; 195:421.

Unhappy Dreams

Kesey K, 2007 (first published 1962). One Flew over the Cuckoo's Nest. Penguin Books.

Ellis J. Why do we dream? The Conversation, 14 April 14 2020 https://theconversation.com/why-do-we-dream-135609

Storr A, 1989. Freud: A Very Short Introduction. Oxford: Oxford University Press.

Fine R, 2013 (first published in 1962). Freud, a Critical Re-evaluation of his Theories. London: Routledge.

Bair D, 2003. Jung: A Biography. New York: Back Bay Books.

British National Formulary, Issue 46. Mehta D (ed). Pharmaceutical Press.

Shuttleworth S. Stress caused sleeplessness for the Victorians too – but they thought it only afflicted 'brain-workers'. The Conversation, 20 September 2019. https://theconversation.com/stress-caused-sleeplessness-for-the-victorians-too-but-they-thought-it-only-afflicted-brain-workers-123247

Shorter E, 1997. A History of Psychiatry. John Wiley and Sons.

Pérusse AD et al., 2016. REM dream activity of insomnia sufferers: a systematic comparison with good sleepers. Sleep Medicine, 20:147-154.

Hall C, 1953. The Meaning of Dreams. New York: Harper and Brothers.

Robbins PR, 2005. The Psychology of Dreams. McFarland & Company.

Foster GM, 1973. Dreams, character, and cognitive orientation in Tzintzuntzan. Ethos, 1:106–121.

Zadra A and Donderi DC, 2000. Nightmares and bad dreams: Their prevalence and relationship to well-being. Journal of Abnormal Psychology, 109:273-281.

Happy Ever After

Duggan A. Reactionaries and Revolutionaries: Classical Fairy Tales and Class. Culture Matters, 19 June 2016. https://culturematters.org.uk/index.php/arts/fiction/item/2327-reactionaries-and-revolutionaries-classical-fairy-tales-and-class

The Editors of Encyclopaedia Britannica. Aesop, legendary Greek fabulist. https://www.britannica.com/biography/Aesop

Edwardes M, Taylor E, trans. (1905). Grimm's Fairy Tales. New York: Maynard, Merrill, & Co.

Maid in Manhattan, 2002. Directed by Wayne Wang, screenplay by Kevin Wade. Columbia Pictures, Revolution Studios.

Pretty Baby, 1990. Directed by Garry Marshall, written by J. F. Lawton. Touchstone Pictures, Silver Screen Partners IV.

La chemise de l'homme heureux: http://conte-du-monde.blogspot.com/2010/01/la-chemise-de-lhomme-heureux-conte_6722.html

von Franz ML, 1996 (first published in 1970). The Interpretation of Fairy Tales. Shambala.

Bair D, 2003. Jung: A Biography. New York: Back Bay Books.

Tolstoy L, 2012 (first published in 1877). Anna Karenina. Vintage.

Paradise Mislaid

Dante Alighieri, 2018 (first published in 1320). The Divine Comedy. e-artnow.

The Editors of Encyclopaedia Britannica. Beatrice: Italian noble. https://www.britannica.com/biography/Beatrice-Italian-noble

Jones J. Bosch's Garden of Earthly Delights shows a world waking up to the future. The Guardian. https://www.theguardian.com/artanddesign/jonathanjonesblog/2017/jan/10/bosch-garden-of-earthly-delights-shows-a-world-waking-up-to-the-future

Museo del Prado. Tríptico del Jardín de las delicias. El Bosco. https://www.museodelprado.es/coleccion/obra-de-arte/triptico-del-jardin-de-las-delicias/02388242-6d6a-4e9e-a992-e1311eab3609

James Hilton, 1999 (first published in 1933). Lost Horizons. Bt Bound.

Wood M. Origins of Shangri-La. BBC History. http://www.bbc.co.uk/history/ancient/cultures/shangri_la_01.shtml

Virgil, Coleman R (ed), 2008: Eclogues (Cambridge Greek and Latin Classics).

Frangou S and Byrne P, 2000. How to manage the first episode of schizophrenia Early diagnosis and treatment may prevent social disability later. BMJ, 321: 522–523.

Loss of Innocence

Weinstein ND, 1980. Unrealistic optimism about future life events. Journal of Personality and Social Psychology, 39:806–820.

Jefferson A et al, 2017. What is unrealistic optimism? Consciousness and Cognition: 50:3–11.

Langer EJ, 1975. The illusion of control. Journal of Personality and Social Psychology, 32:311–328.

Burger JM and Palmer ML, 1992. Changes in and Generalization of Unrealistic Optimism Following Experiences with Stressful Events: Reactions to the 1989 California Earthquake. Personality and Social Psychology Bulletin, 18:39-43.

Hoorens V and Buunk BP, 1993. Social Comparison of Health Risks: Locus of Control, the Person-Positivity Bias, and Unrealistic Optimism. Journal of Applied Social Psychology, 23:291-302.

Alloy CB and Abramson LY 1979. Depressed and nondepressed students: sadder but wiser. Journal of Experimental Psychology, 108: 441-485.

Barak Y et al, 2005. Increased Risk of Attempted Suicide Among Aging Holocaust Survivors. American Journal of Geriatric Psychiatry,13:701-4.
Frankl VE, 2004 (first published in 1959). Man's search for meaning. Rider.
Pytell TE. Redeeming the Unredeemable: Auschwitz and Man's Search for Meaning. Holocaust and Genocide Studies, 2003, 17:89-113.
Levi P, 1976 (first published in 1958). Se questo è un uomo. Turin: Giulio Einaudi Editore.
Levi P, 1988. The Drowned and the Saved. New York: Vintage.

Patchy biographies

Non, je ne regrette rien. Music composed by Charles Dumont. Lyrics by Michel Vaucaire.
My Way. Music based on "Comme d'habitude", by Jacques Revaux. English lyrics by Paul Anka.
Jansari A and Parkin, AJ, 1996. Things that go bump in your life: Explaining the reminiscence bump in autobiographical memory. Psychology and Aging, 11:85–91.
Polkinghorne DE, 1991. Narrative and Self-Concept. Journal of Narrative and Life History, 1:2/3: 135–153.
Polster E, 1987. Every person's life is worth a novel. New York: Norton.
Do AM et al, 2008. Evaluations of pleasurable experiences: The peak-end rule. Psychonomic Bulletin & Review, 15:96–98.
Wildschut T et al, 2006. Nostalgia: Content, triggers, functions. Journal of Personality and Social Psychology, 91:975–993.
Routledge C et al., 2011. The past makes the present meaningful: Nostalgia as an existential resource. Journal of Personality and Social Psychology, 101:638–652.

Burkeman O, 2012. The Antidote. Edinburgh: Cannon Gate.
Storr A, 1989. Freud. Oxford University Press.
Círculo de Poesía. Revista electrónica de literatura. Poemas de Vinicius de Moraes. https://circulodepoesia.com/2013/05/poemas-de-vinicius-de-moraes/
Becker E, 1973. The Denial of Death. New York: Simon & Schuster.
O'Keefe T, 2009. Epicureanism. University of California Press.
Karmel Y. Looking Death in the Eye: Why Your Brain Is Convinced You'll Live Forever. CTECH, 15 November 2019. https://www.calcalistech.com/ctech/articles/0,7340,L-3773483,00.html

How happy should I be?

Lucas Cranach the Elder, 1530. Cupid complaining to Venus. Uffizi Gallery.
Russell JA, 1980. A circumplex model of affect. J. Personal. Social Psychol. 39:1161–1178.
Hunter PG et al., 2010. Feelings and perceptions of happiness and sadness induced by music: Similarities, differences, and mixed emotions. Psychology of Aesthetics, Creativity, and the Arts, 4:47–56.
DuBois TD, 1983. Christian Friedrich Daniel Schubart. Ideen zu Einer Asthetik Der Tonkunst: An Annotated Translation. University of Southern California.
Berrios R et al. Eliciting mixed emotions: a meta-analysis comparing models, types, and measures. Frontiers in Psychology, 15 April 2015. https://doi.org/10.3389/fpsyg.2015.00428
Schneider S and Stone AA, 2015. Mixed emotions across the adult life span in the United States. Psychology and Aging, 30:369–382.
Eco U, 2006 (first published 1994). The Island of the Day Before. Mariner Books.

Popova M. Friedrich Nietzsche on Why a Fulfilling Life Requires Embracing Rather than Running from Difficulty. Brain Pickings. https://www.brainpickings.org/2014/10/15/nietzsche-on-difficulty/

Nietzsche, 1974 (first published in 1882). The Gay Science. Random House.

Hershfield HE et al, 2013. When Feeling Bad Can Be Good: Mixed Emotions Benefit Physical Health Across Adulthood. Social Psychological and Personality Science, 4:54-61.

Notzon S et al, 2017. Modulating Emotion Perception: Opposing Effects of Inhibitory and Excitatory Prefrontal Cortex Stimulation 3(4):329-336.

Help yourself to lashings of happiness

Smiles S, 1859. Self-Help; with illustrations of character and conduct. Ticknor and Fields.

The British Library. Self-Help by Samuel Smiles. https://www.bl.uk/collection-items/self-help-by-samuel-smiles

The Editors of Encyclopaedia Britannica. Émile Coué. https://www.britannica.com/biography/Emile-Coue

Coué E, 2016 (first published in 1920). Self Mastery Through Conscious Autosuggestion & The Practice of Autosuggestion (Including the Study of the Emile Coue's Method & Biography). Kindle Edition. e-artnow

Schwartzman P. How Trump got religion — and why his legendary minister's son now rejects him. Washington Post, 21January 2016.

Newsweek. Religion in 1960 Election. 12/16/07. https://www.newsweek.com/religion-1960-election-95243

Blanton S and Peale NV, 2007. Faith Is the Answer: A Psychiatrist and a Pastor Discuss Your Problems. Kessinger Publishing.

Blanton S, 1971. Diary of my analysis with Freud. New York: Hawthorn.

Ehrenreich B, 2009. Bright-Sided: How the Relentless Promotion of Positive Thinking has Undermined America. Metropolitan Books.

Walker R. Stressed Brits buy record number of self-help books. The Guardian 9 March 2019. https://www.theguardian.com/books/2019/mar/09/self-help-books-sstressed-brits-buy-record-number

Egan-Wyer, C. (2019). The Sellable Self: Exploring endurance running as an extraordinary consumption experience. Lund: Lund University (Media-Tryck).

Egan-Wyer, C. Running: not so much a liberating hobby as a cult. The Conversation, November 27, 2019.

Diagnosis

WHO. WHO remains firmly committed to the principles set out in the preamble to the Constitution. https://www.who.int/about/who-we-are/constitution

Kessler et al, 2002. Detection of depression and anxiety in primary care: follow up study. BMJ, 325:1016.

Cartwright S, 1851. Report of the diseases and peculiarities of the Negro Race. New Orleans Med Surg J., 691-715.

WHO. International Statistical Classification of Diseases and Related Health Problems 10th Revision. https://icd.who.int/browse10/2019/en

Dowrick C, 2009. Beyond depression. 2nd ed. Oxford University Press.

Positive Conclusion (paradoxically)

Oettingen G and Wadden, TA, 1991. Expectation, fantasy, and weight loss: Is the impact of positive thinking always positive? Cogn Ther Res 15:167–175.

Printed in Great Britain
by Amazon

28011031R00110